I0203437

That Shade of Green

Robert Poindexter

Order this book online at www.trafford.com
or email orders@trafford.com

Most Trafford titles are also available at major online book retailers.

© Copyright 2010 Robert Poindexter.
All rights reserved. No part of this publication may be reproduced, stored in a retrieval system, or
transmitted, in any form or by any means, electronic, mechanical, photocopying, recording, or
otherwise, without the written prior permission of the author.

Printed in Victoria, BC, Canada.

ISBN: 978-1-4269-2867-3 (soft)
ISBN: 978-1-4269-2868-0 (hard)

Library of Congress Control Number: 2010903169

*Our mission is to efficiently provide the world's finest, most comprehensive book publishing
service, enabling every author to experience success. To find out how to publish your book, your
way, and have it available worldwide, visit us online at www.trafford.com*

Trafford rev. 08/31/2010

Trafford
PUBLISHING® www.trafford.com

North America & international
toll-free: 1 888 232 4444 (USA & Canada)
phone: 250 383 6864 ♦ fax: 812 355 4082

Foreword

In February 1971, I involuntarily entered the U.S. Army for a two-year tour of duty. I was drafted through the Selective Service System to fulfill my obligation as a citizen and to serve and protect my country. At that time, I had recently graduated from college with a degree in journalism, and I was preparing for a career in the advertising field. I also had some interest in writing feature stories for such magazines as *Reader's Digest* and *National Geographic*.

All of that changed with a single phone call, but I quickly decided to make the best of the situation. I thought it would be interesting to keep a journal of my exploits and experiences while I was in the Army, especially since I was the first member of my family to serve in the military since the Korean Conflict during the 1950s. I kept this journal with the full intention of writing a book sometime in the future. I had no idea that it would take me 40 years to actually finish writing the book, however.

Almost everything that I wrote in my diary is included in this book. I had to omit certain details to protect the privacy of my many friends that I served with in the Army. When my friends found out that I was keeping a journal of our many escapades and that I was intending to actually write a book about it, they all of course wanted to reserve the right to censor the book before it ever went to print. Instead, I agreed to make liberal use of nicknames for them.

You will find as you read that in a lot of cases, I make fun of the military's way of doing things. There are ways to do things, and then there is the "military way." It is an organization unlike any other in the world. But make no mistake, the United States Military is one of the best-run organizations in the world, and many of our enemies have found that out the hard way. While the military has its quirky ways of getting things done, there is a purpose behind everything they do. There are many highly skilled, intelligent, and dedicated people in our military, and without them we Americans would not enjoy the freedoms that we have today.

CHAPTER ONE:

My Story Begins

In 1970, I was a senior at Northern Illinois University and I was living at home with my parents in Aurora, Illinois. Northern is located in the heart of some of the best corn-growing country in both the United States and the world. Our country was in the midst of a turbulent and highly volatile part of our recent history. The Police Action or Vietnam War—whichever you prefer to call it—was in high gear. The United States was in a position just short of total commitment to a war against Communism in Southeast Asia. We were involved in a struggle that put our country under the scrutiny of the rest of the world unequaled since our involvement in World War II and the Korean Conflict.

People in several countries questioned our involvement in Vietnam. Questions even came from within our own country. Many people in the United States didn't believe that we belonged in a fight so far away from home. There are people even to this day who still believe that we were wrong in our foreign policy decisions during this time. One of the big questions being asked by more than a few people was and is, "How could our government rationalize our involvement in a conflict so far from home in a country that had been in turmoil for many years prior to our getting in on the act?"

My own feelings about all of this were pretty well set, even though as a student in a relatively quiet school I was not directly involved in it. I believed during that time that our country had a world commitment to protect those smaller, underdeveloped countries from the threat of a spreading Communist takeover. In my opinion, we had a commitment to preserve the rights of individuals in any country to freedom and liberty from oppressive forms of government. This opinion was based strictly on my studies of our history since becoming a nation, as well as my own feelings about being a freethinking American citizen.

Of course, my opinion on the Vietnam War—or any war for that matter—were easy to formulate since I was about as far away from war and fighting as you could get. Being a student of journalism, I was probably more aware of what was going on in this world than some other students were. And since I have never in my life been an overly shy person about expressing my views on things, I had my opinions on the subject. I found out, however, that I was often in the minority when it came to accepting our involvement in Vietnam. I actually believed that we had good reasons for being in the fight. I never let myself get so overzealous in my views that I would actually fight for them, however. After all, people had their opinions and I had mine about the war. I wasn't about to come to blows to prove my point.

The war in Vietnam continued throughout the school year, and I never really got overly involved with it until the day that my Draft number in Mr. Nixon's now famous Draft Lottery was announced. Until that event took place, I had no inclination that I could possibly end up in Vietnam myself. Then it suddenly dawned on me that I was a prime candidate for the Draft. I had spent four years going to college preparing myself for a future in the business world. I never dreamed that I could possibly get drafted and sent off to a war that was so far away from home. Here I was riding through college on a student deferment for four years, and suddenly that protection was stripped away. And all I had to show for it was this idiotic number.

At the time, Conscription, or "the Draft," as it was more commonly known, was not a new concept in the history of the United States. During the American Revolution, our fledgling states all had the authority from the Constitution to draft men into state militias for protection and to enforce the law. The first time Conscription was used on a national basis was during the American Civil War. The Union Army employed over two million soldiers during that war. Of that number, only 2% were actually drafted. Another 6% of the Union Army was made up of paid substitutes for those who chose not to serve. The Confederate Army started drafting men in 1862. There was widespread resistance to this practice on both sides of the conflict. Therefore, both sides allowed for substitutes to be hired in lieu of being drafted.

The concept of the modern Draft was first introduced in a bill before Congress in 1926. The measure was finally approved into law in 1934. The first peacetime Draft occurred in 1940. By 1942, local Draft Boards were established throughout the country. In 1948 (the year I was born, ironically), Congress passed into law the establishment of the Selective Service Act. This act required all men between the ages of 18 and 26 to register for the Draft.

Throughout the 1960s, the United States became more heavily involved in the war in Vietnam. As time went on, our commitment caused troop strength to increase to combat the increasing insurgency throughout Vietnam. Between 1964 and 1975, approximately 9.2 million men and women served in the military. About 3.2 million of those served in Vietnam. Most of them were men who had been drafted after the Draft Lottery was started in 1969 by then President Richard Nixon. Men were drafted for the war in Vietnam for the last time in 1972. Since that time there has been one attempt to reinstate the Draft, which was in 1986. Since 1986 the newest laws concerning the Selective Service Act allow for both men and women to be drafted into the military if necessary.

My number in the lottery turned out to be 153. At first glance this was not a bad number to get, but it wasn't that great either. All it simply meant was that all of those guys who had lower numbers than 153 would be drafted before me. As it turned out, 153 was passed in the Draft process long before I graduated from college in June 1970. My student deferment got me through until I graduated. But after that, I knew that it would just be a matter of time before the government's bureaucracy caught up with me and put me in the Army.

I remember sitting at my college commencement ceremony enjoying the fact that I had accomplished something in my life. But something kept popping up in my mind that was messing up all of my happy thoughts. I kept thinking, "I'm going to get my little ass drafted!" God, what a horrible thought! In spite of all the pomp and circumstance of the occasion, I really was getting sick to my stomach as each minute passed by that day. The thought that kept going through my head was, "What good is a degree in journalism going to do me when I get myself shot in Vietnam?"

I had some big decisions to make about my life after graduating. Should I just sit around and wait for my Draft notice to come in the mail? Should I look for a job and hope that I could get a work deferment from the Draft? I honestly didn't know what to do. After pushing myself to graduate in four years, I was ready to goof-off for a while. But this Lottery thing had thrown a monkey wrench into the whole scheme of things. At 21 years of age with a college degree in my hands, no debts to repay, being single and unattached, and everything looking toward a bright future, I couldn't decide what to do. I couldn't even decide what kind of work I really wanted to do for the rest of my life. The only thing that I knew for sure was that if I didn't decide soon the Army would decide for me—like it or not.

During that first week after graduation, my parents, like many other people who knew me during this period of my life, had a hard time understanding why I couldn't decide what to do with my life. After all, I was a brilliant college graduate! I had something that neither of my parents had ever been able to get. They, like a lot of other people in our country at the time, believed that all somebody needed to get started on the road to success was a college education. Once you had that, it was simple: Find a job in the area of expertise that you had studied, start out on the ground floor of any type of job, and work your way up the ladder of success. The theory was good enough. After all, thousands of college graduates, including my older brother, had done this very thing and were happy as hell. They couldn't understand why I didn't want to do the same thing.

After several heated discussions at home, my dad finally convinced me that sitting around complaining about everything was no answer for what to do with my life. So I reluctantly started looking for a job. My efforts proved fruitless, however, at least in the field of journalism. Either the money wasn't right or that horrible subject of my Draft status kept getting in the way of any possible job opportunity. Needless to say, I quit pursuing a job in journalism within a week of my graduation from college. This was a lousy way to start the rest of my life.

Undaunted, I still felt that things would work out one way or another; they always had in the past. My situation was not a total loss. During the last two years of my schooling, I had financed my way through it while working for the Burlington Northern Railroad as a locomotive fireman during the summer months. I liked the work, and the money was really great compared to what a lot of people were making in those days. I had originally gotten the job on the railroad with my dad's help. He was a 35-year railroader at the time and a supervisor to boot. He was in a position in which he had some influence on who was hired. With his help, I was hired by the railroad for two straight summers.

With some urging from my parents, I hired out again on the railroad for the third summer in a row. My thoughts at the time were that even though I really didn't want to be a railroader for my career, at least I would have something to do for the summer. I knew that I could make some good money while I waited for the Draft to catch up with me.

A month went by into the summer and I hadn't heard anything from the Draft Board. As the time passed, I became less worried about being drafted and I started making some plans for the future. By mid-summer, I had decided to work for about six months and then return to school in February 1971 to earn a master's degree in business administration. After earning my degree I would again—this time seriously—look for a job in the writing field, maybe in advertising. I finished the summer working, making lots of money, and chasing around while single and fancy-free.

In September 1970, the railroad eliminated all of its summer help except for me. My dad managed to talk my boss into retaining me at the end of the summer on a semi-permanent basis due to my pending Draft status. For this I am eternally grateful to this day. As it turned out, I was able to keep my job on the railroad and my seniority until I returned from the Army two years later.

As for my plans to return to school for the spring semester, it was strictly questionable at this point. I knew that the Draft Board was overdue in catching up with me and that any day I could get one of those "nasty-grams." Besides, it sounded good when I talked with my boss at work. I still had a job strictly on the premise that I would either be returning to school or getting drafted soon. I was really not going to be a permanent fixture on the railroad. I continued to reassure my boss that I was definitely going back to school in February if the Army didn't get to me first. Apparently, upper management was questioning from time to time why I was still working in the fall when I was classified as a full-time student. My boss was receiving pressure off and on to cut my job, and he and my dad had to pull a few strings to keep me on the payroll.

By mid-October 1970, I actually began to believe that the Draft Board had missed me and I was going to be able to return to school. This crazy thought came to an abrupt halt one evening at about 7:30 p.m. I remember the time only because after working until 6:30 p.m., I had arrived at home and had just sat down to one of my mom's usually good home-cooked meals. I was halfway through this fine meal when the telephone rang. The telephone ringing at our house was nothing unusual because of my dad's position on the railroad, so I didn't give it a second thought. He was always getting phone calls at all hours of the evening about derailments and engine problems.

However, this time the call was for me instead of my dad. I knew it couldn't be the railroad because I had just gotten off work and wasn't rested enough to return. I was also pretty sure that it wasn't a girl calling since my love life had been for the most part nil and all zeroes since a serious fling I had had during my senior year of college had fallen apart during the last month of school. I asked who was calling, and my mom said that it was the Draft Board. I just about fell out of my chair! I couldn't believe it! The first thought that ran through my head was that the person on the phone must have been working overtime just to get to little old me. Most government agencies never work past 5 p.m. My D-Day had finally arrived.

I answered the telephone, and a nice and very polite woman on the other end of the line began to systematically grill me about my life history. She asked what seemed like 100 questions about what I was doing now, if I was still in school, and what my future plans included. She said that all of these questions were being asked so she could simply update my file with the Draft Board about my civilian status. I, of course, emphasized that although I wasn't presently in school, my intentions were to return there in the near future. The very nice and polite lady said nothing to all of my astounding proclamations except "OK."

At the end of our conversation she asked for my current address and told me that she would be sending out a small questionnaire that I was to fill out and return to the Draft Board. She suggested quite strongly that I fill this out promptly and return it as soon as possible. I thought to myself, "Do the orders start already? I'm not even in the Army yet and they're giving me orders!" I didn't dare ask what would happen if I didn't fill out the damn thing. Instead like any other well-bred jerk, I politely said that I would fill it out quickly. I actually thanked her for calling. I'm not sure exactly what I was thankful for, but I was always taught to thank people for calling me.

Well, after a hard day on the railroad and this lovely telephone call, I found it hard to finish my meal. I didn't sleep well that night either. Even going to bed late combined with several beers didn't abate my anxiety over this whole sordid affair. I just couldn't believe that the Draft Board worked overtime to get to me, "Joe College," ace journalism major. I was sure that the Army had plenty of men and that they really didn't need a guy like me in their ranks. After all, I had never shot a gun in my life! Although I was in pretty good shape and fairly good at sports, I had never been able to run a mile in one stretch. I was never known to be mechanically oriented—I couldn't even keep my car running on a regular basis. At that time in my life the things that I couldn't do far outweighed the things that I could do. Why would the Army want a jerk like me?

To make matters worse, the questionnaire that I was to receive in a few days arrived the next afternoon. Those Draft people even had the audacity to put a deadline on it for when the damn thing had to be returned. I am amazed to this day how efficient our government was in this matter. In my three college courses of political science, I never read once that our federal government was ever praised for its efficiency in handling correspondence. In my case the Draft Board should have received the Medal of Honor for its efficiency. They definitely had my number!

Within one week, my Draft status went from 2S (student, not draft-able) to 1A (single, unattached male—highly draft-able). Exactly one week from the day that I returned that stupid questionnaire, I was holding my notice for a physical examination for entry into the Armed Forces. I was to go into Chicago in late- December 1970 for this physical. This gave me about a month to figure out some way that I wasn't physically fit for duty in the Army. And since I was feeling fine, I saw no way to get around my pending Draft status for the good of my country.

I must insert here that at this time I felt that I was as good and patriotic as the next guy, but I still didn't think too much about getting drafted. In fact, I thought it was a terrible idea. I could already see myself wading in some rice paddy, which is basically a ditch or a field of ditches full of water in which they grow rice plants. The rice paddy I envisioned was full of snake-infested stinking water, and I was ducking bullets that were spraying over my head. This was not my idea of a good time.

So I spent the next month figuring out ways to flunk my physical. One idea was to be underweight, which I thought would have been easy to accomplish since I wasn't very large to begin with. At the time, I was about 5'5" and weighed about 125 pounds. By simply starving myself and not drinking any more beer I could easily drop enough weight and go into my physical looking like a starved waif from some poor underdeveloped nation. This idea passed quickly, however, since I realized that I would have to lose about 30 pounds to be underweight by the Army's standards. Besides, my mother would never approve of starving myself while I was still living at home. No mother in her right mind would do this—especially my mother—even even to keep her kid from being drafted. And I just couldn't give up the beer anyway. In fact, after receiving the notice for my physical my beer intake went up and I gained an additional pound prior to my physical in December.

My second idea was to go for insanity. I would go into the physical and do a bunch of crazy things and giggle all the time in hopes that the good Army doctors would let me go as a totally unacceptable form of human existence. This idea also quickly went by the wayside. I was far too intelligent of a person to do something like that, and I never was any good at acting anyway.

Going for being overweight was entirely out of the question. I had spent 21 years gorging myself, especially in college, to get to the 125 pounds that I weighed at the time. After graduating from high school at a powerful 105 pounds of pure dynamite, it took four years of extra meals, pizza, Italian beef sandwiches, and beer parties to gain 20 extra pounds and grow four inches in height. Weight gain has never been one of my better skills.

After mulling over several other irrational ideas on how to avoid the Army, I had but one alternative left in my arsenal of thoughts. During my senior year in college I had a tumor develop on my right ankle and I had to have surgery to remove it. The surgery took out about half of my bone along with the tumor, so for months I was in a cast until the bone grew back into place. This caused me to have a slightly weak right ankle for some time. It had been less than a year since the surgery, and if I thought really hard I could feel pain in my ankle.

With this inspiration, I went back to the University just prior to my Army physical and met with the bone doctor who had done the surgery. I explained my predicament to him and asked him to take an X-ray of my ankle to see if it had healed OK. I, of course, was hoping for the worst. As it turned out, my ankle was perfect and the surgery had been a success. In fact, the only sign of the operation at all was a three-inch scar on my leg. I did, however, get the doctor to write a letter recommending that I not participate in extreme walking or marching activities. Therefore, I left the good doctor's office feeling that I had a slim chance of not being accepted into the military.

All of my good thoughts collapsed on the day of my physical. I took the physical and passed with flying colors. A perfect human specimen! The only thing that was detected during this six-hour nightmare of standing in lines and answering stupid questions in my birthday suit was that one doctor thought he heard a slight heart murmur and asked me if anyone had ever mentioned this before. I couldn't recall that anyone had, so that little notation went by the wayside. As to my letter from the orthopedic surgeon, the Army boys simply took the letter without reading it and stuck it in my file with my other test results.

The final results of my physical examination found me to be in excellent health without exception. The final approving doctor told me the results while I stood in front of him in my BVD's holding the rest of my clothes. He told me that there was nothing he could see in my physical results that would change my 1A Draft status. This news was bad enough, but he didn't stop there. What he said next just about made me drop my clothes that I desperately needed to put back on to keep from freezing to death. His next sentence made me forget that I had been cold and highly embarrassed for six hours during this superb U.S. Government physical. This friendly and somewhat sympathetic doctor told me that I would have approximately four to six weeks before I would be inducted into the Army. This news just thrilled me to no end. He might as well have stabbed me right there on the spot. Then he actually had the nerve to smile and wish me good luck.

I came home on the train in total silence and definitely in a lousy mood. My only good thought was that I wasn't the only one who had passed the physical that day. Several hundred other guys of varying sizes and shapes had passed too. My days of carefree living were coming to an end. It almost felt like I had been told that I only had four to six weeks to live. I certainly hadn't done everything that I had wanted to do in my life yet. Patriotic as I was, I really didn't relish the thought of risking my life and limb in defense of my country at the tender age of 21. After all, I had just reached the legal drinking age and I hadn't even voted yet. All I could say to anyone was, "This is a bunch of shit!"

All this time I thought I was living in a democracy where everybody got their say on things having to do with their lives. Nobody, ever once, since this whole affair started in mid-October asked for my opinion on whether I agreed with all of this or not. I was ordered to fill out the questionnaire, I was ordered to take the physical, and I was about to be ordered to enter the Army. I thought those people who say that things could be worse obviously had never been in this situation before. I have to admit that this was one of the low points in my life. Even my breakup with my college flame didn't bother me as much as getting drafted. While I never considered it myself, I could understand why many young men during this time elected to avoid the Draft and leave the country. Each person had to live with his or her decisions and I was willing to go with mine. I thought I might as well take the Draft and make the most of it.

I was at work the next day, but my worries about the Army were still weighing heavily on my mind. I continued worrying until lunchtime, which was when the strangest thought popped into my head. I had been saving money for school all of this time, and now it was just going to sit there for two years or maybe for forever. The question was, should I just leave the money there in the bank to collect interest for my future or should I spend it? After some thought on this matter I came up with a compromise. I decided to do something that I had always wanted to do, which was travel on my own. I wouldn't need all of the money to do this. I could save some of it for the future.

After work, I sat down and figured out my total working time on the railroad during the past six months. I found out that I had accumulated enough time to earn a weeklong vacation with pay effective January 1, 1971. With a little maneuvering on my part, I later talked my boss into letting me take the first week in January as vacation time. I decided to wait a few days before making my grand plan for my future general knowledge. On December 29, 1970, I broke the news to my parents.

I saved my grand announcement until dinner that evening. We were all seated at the table having a nice, quiet meal. My parents were about to devour some apple pie when I announced my grand plan. I stated that on January 1, I was intending to go to the Bahamas for a week of vacation. Everyone stopped eating, and the looks on my parents' faces were really quite interesting. My mother was speechless for one of the very few times in her life. My father, lifting his usually non-committal eyes, said, "That's only two days from now." After some discussion about the intelligence of my decision and the possible expense of such a trip, I was still convinced that my decision to take it was absolutely bordering on brilliance.

Therefore, on January 1, 1971, I headed for the Bahamas. I spent four days and three nights in this beautiful paradise. I did everything you can imagine in those few days, including renting a Honda motorbike and riding around the islands to secluded beaches, going to the casinos at night, and flirting with every attractive girl I could get to talk to me. The trip cost me nearly $1000, but it was worth every penny.

Upon my return from the Bahamas, I went back to work to wait out the time before I received that wonderful letter from the Draft Board. I was working the midnight shift so I always got the first crack at the mail every morning. However, as things go on the railroad, I was called to work on a Saturday morning before the mail arrived. I immediately took this as a bad sign since every day before that I had been retrieving the mail and happily not coming up with any letters. As I had expected, the omen came true. I had a break in the afternoon and called home to check on the mail. My mother told me that I had received two letters—one from the Graduate School of Business at Northern Illinois University, and the other from the U.S. Government. The former was my acceptance letter into the Graduate School of Business, and the latter was my Draft Notice.

I was thrilled to learn that I was ordered to report to the AFEES Building in Chicago on the morning of February 9, 1971 at 6:00 a.m. for induction into the U.S. Armed Services. As it turned out, this ended up being less than one week before I would have been safely back in school continuing my education. This is a small fact that I still regret because I never accomplished my goal when I returned two years later from the Army. I don't really know whether this would have made a difference in my life, but it is one of many things that I started out to do and never finished. I have resolved, however, that life on this earth has many challenges. Being human, I'm allowed a few errors in judgment. That is what makes life interesting for all of us, right?

In any case, over the next two weeks I made it a point to see all of my friends from school and invite them to a party that I had decided to throw in honor of my entrance into the Army. Not that I was happy with this idea, but since it was inevitable why not celebrate it? So on February 6, 1971, I had my last big fling as a civilian for the next two years. And as might be expected, I drank myself silly!

CHAPTER TWO:

The First Day

Following the schedule set forth in the letter from my favorite "uncle," I arose early on the morning of February 9, 1971. To be more precise, it was 4:00 a.m., which is an absolutely un-Godly hour of the morning to get out of bed. I went to the kitchen and found both of my parents already sitting at the table over steaming cups of coffee. They both looked half-awake as most people do at 4:00 a.m. I aimed for the coffee pot myself and then sat down with them. For the next 15 or 20 minutes, we all just sat there staring at our coffee cups and saying absolutely nothing, which was highly unusual at our house. There are very few times that I can remember during my life at home when nobody had anything to say. You wouldn't believe the number of worldly problems that we "solved" over the years. We Poindexter's are well-known for being authorities on just about everything.

After about 20 minutes of total silence, I couldn't stand it anymore. I finally said, "Well?" (Very profound, wouldn't you say?) My mother was instantly in tears and became very emotional about my leaving for the Army. As usual, my dad just sat there with nothing to say. After this brilliant beginning, my parents and I talked over all of the last-minute suggestions and plans that we had been making during the past few days. I forced down my last civilian breakfast and then hurried off to the bathroom to shower and shave. Whether I liked it or not, my civilian life was coming to an end in short order. I reluctantly finished packing one small suitcase holding a few changes of clothes, underwear, socks, toiletries, and a few personal items while getting ready to go to my new home-away-from-home—the U.S. Army. I wasn't sure that I was ready for this dramatic change in my life.

At approximately 5:30 a.m., my dad and I shuffled out to my car and headed for the Northwestern Railroad train station in nearby Geneva, Illinois. This fact even bothered me on this particular morning. Here I was an employee of the Burlington Northern Railroad, and I was being forced to ride on a competing line into Chicago to of all things enter the Army! The only good thing about the whole deal was that the ride was free. But I wasn't impressed.

Being good railroaders, we were of course early in our arrival to the train station. My dad and I sat in the car talking about the railroad and anything but the Army. Unfortunately, the train was on time. It was finally time to go to where my fate had led me. I said goodbye and told my dad that I would probably get some leave time in about eight weeks. Hopefully, I would have time to come home for a short stay between Basic Training and Advanced Training. At this point, however, I didn't even know where I was going for the first stage of my illustrious Army career.

After about an hour's ride through the suburbs on a typically cold February day, our train, which was packed full of new recruits and a few early-rising business people, arrived at the Northwestern Railroad terminal station in Chicago. After getting off the train with the rest of my newly found comrades from the suburbs, we found out that the building that we were supposed to report to was eight blocks away. In fact, it was closer to the Burlington Northern station in Chicago than it was to the one we came into. We all concluded immediately that this was nothing short of pure harassment. My first thoughts were, "Here I am marching already for miles and I'm not even officially sworn-in yet!" About 50 of us walked as a group to the AFEES Building. After an eight-block walk in the Chicago wind tunnel commonly referred to as the "Loop," we as a group were glad for some refuge in the nearest warm building.

Once inside the AFEES Building, we all began thawing out. After a couple of minutes of pure confusion as to where to go next we found our way to the entrance area. We entered a large room filled with cheap government-issue metal seats. There was nothing terribly unusual about the room except for the floor. It was covered with red lines and arrows leading out through another door into the hallway that we had just come through. It was now about 7:15 a.m. We stood around for a few minutes still trying to thaw out from the frigid weather outside.

Gradually, the noise level in the room rose as a few of the hotshots in the group started kidding around and cracking jokes about the fix we were all in. How anyone could have a sense of humor about getting drafted and standing in a cold room with little red arrows all over the floor was beyond me! I actually was laughing at some of the comments. They weren't funny, but it helped keep my nerves on an even keel.

A short time later, a burly three-striper sergeant came in and told us to sit down and reduce the noise to a college roar. After an additional hour's wait, we were ushered into the exam area and were ordered to strip to our shorts and prepare ourselves for our induction physical. This was done alphabetically. With my name starting with a "P," I of course had to wait for all of the "A's" through "O's" to go first.

It was here that I think I first caught a cold. I sat there in my shorts holding the rest of my clothes in a room that couldn't have been over 60 degrees for another 45 minutes. I was thinking during this wait that either these guys in the Army were a bunch of health nuts, or they hadn't paid their heating bill for the month of January and the gas company had turned off the heat in the building. I really didn't care which of these assumptions were correct; all I knew was that I felt ridiculous without my clothes on. If you can imagine, here I was sitting in a room with several other guys. We were all in our shorts just looking around trying to look perfectly natural. What a sight to behold!

My turn finally arrived and I stepped up to the first desk. The clerk behind the desk thumbed through his records and found my file. He reviewed with me all of my vital statistics and verified that all of the information was true and correct. I was too cold to disagree with anything he said, so I presume everything checked out. When he was finished he handed me the file and directed me to follow the red arrows on the floor to begin the physical. I was off and running following the arrows. I went through the various exam stations as fast as I could. I wasn't in a hurry, mind you, but since I was freezing to death I thought it would get me into my clothes faster.

I hit all of the usual stations, including the one where the joker stands there and orders you to bend over and spread your cheeks. After doing this, he walks down the line of naked guys declaring each individual as either "active" or "inactive," and he is trailed by another guy with a clipboard writing all of this pertinent information down. Being a highly intelligent college graduate, it took me only a couple of minutes to figure out what the hell they meant by active or inactive: active meant you had had a recent bowel movement, and inactive meant you hadn't. Some of the other dummies in the crowd never did figure it out though. They thought it was funny. A few jerks down the line from me spent the whole time bent over snickering and making complete asses (pun intended) out of themselves. It's amazing how human beings react to embarrassing situations. Some of us more intelligent people handle this kind of thing quite well, while others behave like untrained wild monkeys.

After about three hours of examinations, I was pronounced to be in generally good health and was directed to the dining area to have lunch prior to the Induction Ceremony. It was now about 11:45 a.m. I ate lunch in silence and solitude, simply enjoying the fact that I once again had my clothes on. My first meal in the Army was so tasty that I don't recall what it consisted of.

At around 1:00 p.m., the original group of guys that I came in with that morning began closing ranks and assembling together at one end of the dining area. The same burly sergeant who had greeted us earlier in the day came up and directed us into a rather nice-looking room with rich blue carpeting covering the floor. Outside of the carpeting, only one other object in the room caught my eye. On the wall in the front of the room was a large U.S. Government Seal. I determined that this must be where we were going to be officially sworn into the Army.

My intuition was correct. After milling around for a few minutes waiting on a few stragglers from the dining area to arrive, another husky and slightly overweight sergeant marched in and yelled at us to cut the noise and line up in rows in alphabetical order. Now this would seem to be an easy task to most people, but you wouldn't believe the total confusion that this simple order caused in this group. It was like trying to get off a crowded subway when everyone else was trying to get on.

We inspired recruits managed to get this so screwed up that we all had to leave the room and come back in as our names were called, which took an extra 15 minutes. By this time our induction leader was so pissed off that he ordered complete silence in the room. So we all stood there in our neat little rows for an additional 15 minutes doing absolutely nothing. During this last 15-minute stint, I must have dissected every corner of the U.S. Government Seal in my mind at least 10 times. Finally, "Sergeant Asshole" came back into the room and decided that we were behaving well enough to join the Army.

For the next few minutes we received our instructions for the upcoming Induction Ceremony. For some reason I couldn't concentrate on what the old boy was saying. One thing I did remember about his instructions was that we were supposed to keep our eyes directly to the front of the room at all times. We had to do this no matter what happened and no matter who came in the room. Outside of this, I didn't remember anything else. The only reason that I remembered this much was because this jerk repeated this same line about 20 times in the 10 minutes or so that he talked to the group.

The actual Induction Ceremony went rather smoothly considering our earlier fiasco of trying to line up correctly. I must say that we handled ourselves quite well. By approximately 2:00 p.m., we were all part of the New Action Army. Our new designation was "trainee." After the oath was administered, we were then directed into a large waiting room already occupied by several other new recruits. We were told that we could now make a telephone call if we wished, or we could do whatever else we wanted to do as long as we didn't leave the area.

I sat down with a couple of guys who had come in on the same train as I had that morning. We talked over our morning's activities, which seemed like the most interesting topic we could think of to discuss at the time. But after a short time, we ran out of topics to talk about and we all ended up just sitting there watching everyone else do the same thing.

At around 3:00 p.m., yet another sergeant came in and announced that everyone in my group would be going to Fort Campbell, Kentucky for our Basic Training. He also stated that we would be loading onto buses shortly and that nobody was to leave the room. His idea of "shortly" lasted another hour before they herded us down the hallways and several flights of stairs to the basement of the AFEES Building. Standing outside the basement doors were several buses waiting to be loaded. During the next 30 minutes, we boarded the buses with our luggage in a systematic, alphabetical order. They crammed us in the buses tightly and with little regard for anyone's comfort.

By 5:00 p.m. and after sitting cooped up in tight quarters for another 30 minutes, we blasted off for Kentucky. We on Bus No.1 had been graciously supplied with a box lunch of cold fried chicken, a roll, and a can of pop just prior to leaving the AFEES Building. Sitting on a crowded bus with my suitcase jammed on the floor under my feet and a box lunch in my lap was certainly not my idea of First Class travel quarters, but I was in no position to complain. I just sat there looking out the window at the fading lights of the Chicago skyline with my elbow in my seat partner's ribs and his in mine.

So this was the way it was in the New Action Army. If the last 10 hours were any indication of what was in store for the next two years, I just couldn't wait to see what happened next. Forcing us to get up at 4:00 in the morning was ridiculous. We could have waited until at least 6:00—a much more civilized hour of the day. After all, how much can you do in the dark when you are only half-awake? Then they made us ride a train that brought us into Chicago to a railroad station that was eight blocks from where we were supposed to report. We could have just taken a train that would have brought us into the city six blocks closer to our destination. And we were put through a second complete physical exam that we had just had six weeks earlier. Since all of us were between the ages of 18 and 26, how much could have changed in our health status in six weeks? And standing around in your underwear for long periods of time in a cold room can't be healthy for anyone. We did a lot of this as time went on. We were treated like a herd of lost sheep. Every move we made was as a group.

From the first few hours of my time in the Army, I was already getting the idea that the powers-that-be assumed that nobody knew anything and they had to teach you everything. And in order for them to be satisfied that everybody was getting it they repeated the instructions over and over again. As I would soon find out, it did no good to get finished early with anything because if you did, they simply made you wait until everyone else was done before proceeding to the next assignment.

The next seven hours of this day went by rather uneventfully, possibly because we were all starting to feel the effects of getting up at 4:00 a.m. In any case, I was a little surprised by how fast the time rolled by while we were stuffed in this bus going on and on down the highway at a high rate of speed. The Army officials in Chicago had done a brilliant job of loading us and assigning us to buses. By putting us on the buses in alphabetical order, they managed to mix up several different groups of recruits into one very large one. This way there was little possibility of knowing anyone.

Bus No. 1 had a strange mix of young and older (I was one of the older ones at age 22) men, some from the affluent suburbs, as well as some from probably the worst ghettos in the Chicago area. I personally wasn't bothered by this melting pot idea, but there were definitely some tough-looking guys on this bus. The only thing we all had in common was that we were all draftees from the Chicago area on our way to good old Dixieland for our Basic Training.

Now I still do not know the distance from Chicago to Fort Campbell, Kentucky, but I'm willing to bet that our bus driver made the trip in record time. The whole trip from downtown Chicago to the front gate of Fort Campbell lasted a total of less than seven hours, including a 15-minute stop somewhere in southern Indiana. The bus driver must have been scared that one of us would jump ship or hijack the damned thing. He never slowed down below 70 mph all the time we were moving unless he absolutely had to.

Considering the fact that we were all draftees, I felt that we behaved rather well on the bus. There was plenty of noise, laughter at dirty jokes, and the like, but we didn't mess the bus up or anything. We even left all of the windows, doors, and seats intact. In light of the fact that none of us really wanted to be in this situation, I thought our behavior was very commendable.

When I first heard that our final destination was going to be somewhere in Kentucky, I tried to be as optimistic as I could under the circumstances. I thought well, at least I'll be going somewhere warmer than Chicago for the rest of the winter. This idea turned out like most of my previous thoughts about the military, however—all screwed up! Arriving around midnight, we drove to the front gate of the Fort in a blinding snowstorm. The bus driver got out of the bus, went up to the guard station, and returned to the bus about five minutes later. At this point, he uttered more than he had said during the entire trip. He announced that it was 10 degrees outside with a windchill of less than zero, and we were to stay on the bus for a while. I couldn't believe it!

Here we were, just 50 miles north of Nashville, Tennessee in the heart of the South and we were still freezing to death. Making matters worse, thanks to our brilliant and highly efficient bus driver's less-than-seven-hour driving performance, we ended up sitting outside the gate for another hour waiting on the other buses to arrive from Chicago. The official word was that the whole Chicago group of trainees had to go into the Fort at the same time for organizational reasons. These reasons were never explained to us, but I'm sure they would not have made sense anyway.

Sometime after 1:00 a.m., the other Chicago buses showed up at Fort Campbell's front gate. I'm not clear as to what time it was since I dozed for a while. I had nothing else to do on that wretched bus. After their arrival, the buses carried us through the gate and on to the reception building near the entrance to the Fort. I still fail to understand why we couldn't have gone to this building to begin with upon our arrival. We could have waited for the others to arrive in a nice, warm, and obviously roomier place than on that stupid bus. But the Army didn't see it that way. It must have made too much sense. Some people are blind to the obvious and the logical.

I really do not recall what exactly the reception building looked like. All that I can remember is entering the building and going by a bunch of desks with clerks at each one. Here they either checked your name off of a manifest or handed you forms to fill out. Then we were escorted into a large room the size of a high school gym, and we sat on the floor filling out all of the forms.

My next mistake was thinking that after all of this hassle and traveling in the last 21 hours that these people would let us finally get some rest. Instead, we spent the next five hours filling out forms. The only benefit that I received from this was that I knew how to spell my name correctly, which I already was an expert at. Although the forms were very simple to fill out and in most cases self-explanatory, you would be amazed at how difficult this task became for some of these guys from Chicago. As the night wore on, I began to wonder if I was the only one in the room who could speak understandable English and write legibly.

At around 8:00 a.m. the following morning, this crazy day finally came to an end. I'm not sure how many forms we filled out—I lost count somewhere after 15. We were then split up into smaller groups, given a pillow and a blanket, and were marched off to our assigned barracks. After being up for around 28 hours, the floor looked good to me. However, since the Army stresses mental and physical stamina, we trudged for what seemed like miles to the billeting (lodging) area in a very rag-tag fashion. For the first time since taking the Oath of Allegiance to protect and defend our country some 18 hours ago, the military establishment didn't pay any attention to how we made our way to our assigned sleeping quarters. I figured that maybe they were half human after all.

Our temporary barracks looked like they had been in existence for quite some time. They were WWII vintage metal huts with rounded roofs made out of corrugated steel. The windows were filthy, and the interior was even worse inside the hut that I, along with some 20-odd new trainees, was assigned to. The beds were in deplorable condition and the mattresses looked overused and grimy. However, I was too tired to complain. I found the first unoccupied cot, dropped my stuff on the floor, put the pillow on the bed, covered myself with a blanket that smelled of moth balls, and fell fast asleep. The next thing that I recall was waking up at around 5:00 p.m. wondering why I had forgotten to take my shoes off. When I looked around, I found out that I wasn't the only one in the group who had forgotten.

After cleaning up and changing into something more presentable, I came out of the lavatory just in time to be enlightened about some Post regulations that were being offered to our group by our new trainee leader. Each group, which was assigned by what hut they slept in, had a trainee leader. This role was usually assigned to an E-4 or specialist-level member of the Headquarters Company. These guys were for the most part pretty easygoing, and we flunkies could ask them just about anything that we wanted to know. Our leader told us about the Post's do's and don'ts, how to get to the PX store, and when and where to eat. He also told us that we would be in this Transient Company for a few days while we were assigned our military clothing and the like.

After completing this phase of our entry into the Army, we would then be assigned to our Basic Training Company for the balance of our stay at Fort Campbell. After answering a few questions, he told us that we had the rest of the evening off to get our feet on the ground. But he cautioned us that we should get plenty of rest because he would be back in the morning at 0430 to shag us out of bed for the next day's activities.

This ended my first full day in the New Action Army. I was still pooped from the previous day and the trip down from Chicago. Outside of the fact that I was sure that I was coming down with a cold, I felt that I had survived the initial blows that Army life had to offer. I could see that my days would be long and my nights would be short in this new life, but I was bound and determined to do the best that I could under the conditions as they came along. As I went to sleep at around 10:00 p.m. on February 10, 1971, I wondered what they would do to us next. I couldn't imagine what we could do at 4:30 in the morning. That was way too early, even for breakfast!

CHAPTER THREE:

You is In the Army Now!

In February, 0430 comes very early. In fact, it's still dark outside. It seems like you never went to bed in the first place. Personal navigation at this time of day is out of the question. Someone has to point you in the right direction just to find the floor. But the Army seems to find no problem with this. They have this funny idea that people can function normally and intelligently early in the morning. I still question this theory. I've never seen anyone fly out of a dead sleep at 4:30 in the morning and be able to function normally and make intelligent decisions. Simple tasks of normal human behavior become next to impossible.

That nice easygoing guy that I mentioned earlier who filled us in on where to go and what to do in the Transient Company transformed into a tyrant the next morning. At the assigned hour he came slamming into our barracks screaming at the top of his lungs to get our trainee asses out of bed and hit the floor! We were informed at this same conversational tone that we had exactly 15 minutes to get our "shit" together and get outside to march to the Mess Hall.

My first official Army breakfast was something in itself to write about. As might be expected, we had to walk several blocks by civilian standards just to get to the Mess Hall. How the name "Mess Hall" came into existence I don't know. After arriving at this Fort's version of the dining hall, I began using my imagination to derive the original roots of the term. The building itself was not very messy, but the way the Army approached the idea of dining was in my mind a true mess. In fact, the whole process reminded me of my early childhood days in grade school. I attended several grade schools when I was a kid because my dad was transferred a lot with the railroad. Because of this, I had the opportunity to see several different lunchrooms and approaches to get little kids to eat balanced meals away from home. I feel that I am somewhat of an expert on this particular subject.

We were told to get into line and go through cafeteria-style past the servers. We were given no choice on what to eat or what not to eat. You simply went through the line and took whatever the servers put on your slotted tray. Of course, nobody made you eat what he or she gave you, but it was highly suggested by our trainee leader that we should take advantage of this glorious opportunity since it would be quite a while before we would have our next meal. He wasn't kidding—lunch didn't come that day until well after noon.

Now, getting up early has never been a big problem for me. Working on the railroad for three summers and getting up for 8:00 a.m. classes in school, etc., got me used to the idea of making the most out of your day by rising early in the morning. Eating at 5:00 a.m. is another thing altogether. To this day, I still have trouble getting out of bed early in the morning and eating right away. I would think that a lot of you could relate to this feeling. I mean, a cup of coffee is fine but certainly not a full and heavy breakfast. Full breakfasts are for about 9:00 or 10:00 in the morning after you've been up for a while and are navigating on all of your burners. Not in the Army though! You eat at the assigned hour and you eat what they give you or you don't eat at all. This was one of many civilian habits I was going to have to break if I was to survive for the next two years. The U.S. Army was simply not into continental breakfasts in 1971. They may be nowadays, but I'm not going back in to find out.

If you have not had powdered eggs, powdered milk, and fake bacon, you really haven't experienced one of the true gourmet delights that mankind has to offer. We did have real toast, but it was either hard from sitting out too long, burnt, or both. What really ticked me off about this fantastic breakfast at 5:00 a.m. on February 11, 1971, was that coffee was not available to the trainees. Only the regular cadre guys could get coffee with their breakfasts. Apparently the Army, in all of its wisdom, determined that "kids" didn't drink coffee and that it was unhealthy anyway.

Using this brilliant logic, the Army probably also figured that it was one of the system's goals to make us all into MEN. Only men drink coffee. This logic was derived from the thought that anyone going into the Army was just a kid. I will agree that a good percentage of the guys I was around at this time were pretty young, and many of them were rather immature in their thoughts and activities. However, there were a few of us around who knew how to eat neatly and put our napkins on our laps. Some of us even knew that food was for eating and not for throwing at each other. By the time the Army had me in the fold, I had been drinking coffee on a regular basis for several years. It was pure and simple horror not being able to have some in my cup in the morning. This "kid" didn't like the system already, and I was only in it for the second full day.

One of the other quirks about this Mess Hall was that you couldn't discuss the time of day or the food while you were in the building. They actually had "heavies" strolling around ensuring that you ate in complete silence. If anyone was talking—even asking for the salt—and was caught by one of these guys he was rudely escorted outside for an "attitude adjustment." By the way, the most common form of attitude adjustment in Basic Training was the all-American push-up. I'll discuss this later in the book, but I will say for now that it was an effective deterrent to abnormal behavior. Some of the morons who I went into the Army with went through several of these attitude adjustments just learning how to eat properly during those first few days of Army life.

After our leisurely 10-minute breakfast we were all hustled outside into the cold—only to stand around and wait for everybody else in the Company to finish eating. This included our trainee leaders, who took their time having an extra cup of coffee and a cigarette if they liked. After all, our next destination for the day, the Supply Hut, didn't open until 6:00 a.m. But of course we didn't know this at the time. They only told you things one at a time so as not to confuse anyone.

Confusion set in anyway since I couldn't figure out why I had to stand outside in the cold while everybody finished eating. After all, there was plenty of room inside the building to house not only our little band of merry trainees but also several other bands as well. I found out rather quickly that this was one area that was not open for discussion. You didn't question the system—you survived it.

Standardization has always been and probably will always be one of the great hallmarks of the U.S. Army. The year 1971 brought nothing new to change this situation. As I mentioned earlier, our next stop for the day was the Supply Depot. This was probably the finest example of standardization that I have ever seen in my life. Some high-ranking official, many years before I was even born I'm sure, made the determination that everyone in the Army must look and dress exactly the same except for the markings of their rank. This was truly a genius-level decision. That same guy must have determined that everybody was the same height, weight, and wears the same size hat and shoes. At least it seemed that way when it came time to receive our clothing from our friendly Supply folks.

One of the forms from our first day at Fort Campbell came back to haunt me at the Supply Depot. If you'll remember, we were required to fill out several forms during the early hours of the morning directly after riding a bus for about seven hours. All of us had been up for at least 20 hours before we ever started filling out any of these forms. Now unless you are superhuman, everyone gets tired after being awake for 20 hours. In fact, one can border on incoherency after being up for that long. While I was careful when I filled out the forms, I along with most of the others made several errors on the paperwork. I was unaware of this until it came time for the Army to issue my clothing.

At precisely 0600 hours Military Time, our group of trainees was poised and in position for our attack on the Supply Depot at Fort Campbell, Kentucky. However, like most everything else in the Army standing in long lines became the order of the day. Again, the assignment of our clothing was handled by the time-honored method of alphabetical order. This meant, of course, that I was in for another long wait to get anything accomplished. After about an hour or so, I was finally in position to cross the threshold into the new world of the Supply Depot, Fort Campbell-style.

As I entered the building housing the Supply Depot the first thought that crossed my mind was, "I wonder if they have my size in clothes?" Now ordinarily, nobody worries about this sort of thing. However, being of a rather slight build for most of my life, this is one thing that has always been a problem for me. I have found over the years that not even the biggest stores in the United States are prepared to fit a guy with a 28-inch inseam and 32-inch arms, armpit to fingertips. So it was no wonder that I would be more than a little bit concerned about this situation. I mean after all, if Sears and Montgomery Ward can't fit you, who can? Oh I could get clothes there, but never in the men's department. It is sometimes hard on your ego to find out that there are actually 10- and 12-year-olds who are bigger than you!

I started down the long counter to each section of the Supply Depot with high hopes that the Army would certainly take into account that every guy is not built the same way. First came the pants section. I found out here that my brilliant job of filling out that form that I mentioned earlier came into play. I had said that I could wear a 30-inch waistline. No problem, the Army had lots of guys with 30-inch waists. I also said "short" on the length. Well, the Army's version of short and my version of short were at least two inches different.

After receiving my issue of two pairs of work pants and two pairs of dress khaki pants, I took the time to hold one of each up to my waist to check on the length. In each case the cuffs were laying on the floor. The specialist handling the pants section assured me that this would be no problem since there was a tailor in the PX complex. All I needed to do was take the pants to him and have them altered to the proper length. I said "great" and went on to the next station. I was thinking though about what I would do in the meantime. Would I go without pants?

I knew that the Army was funny in a lot of ways, but I really didn't think that they would be humored by me standing in my first formation without any pants on. I wouldn't do it anyway. After all, I didn't know who I was going to be standing next to in the formation yet and you never know about people sometimes. Besides, after just one day in the Army my opinion of their screening process of individuals who they thought were fit for the Service was not too high. I had actually seen guys on the bus ride down to Fort Campbell with knives big enough to start a small war.

And from what I could see they were quite adept on the use of them. If the Army took in thugs and juvenile delinquents they probably accepted perverts as well.

I faired a little better in the shirt department. They actually had shirts to fit my specifications. My hopes began to grow again. The colors offered didn't allow for any imagination, but at least they appeared that they would fit. At this stop we received 10 shirts: six long-sleeved work shirts, two long-sleeved dress shirts, and two short-sleeved khaki shirts. A comment must be made here in favor of the Army. They issue, without a doubt, the most durable shirts in the industry. As I write this I still have in my possession many of the shirts that I was originally issued in February 1971. They have lasted at least 25 years now, and some are still in fairly good condition. The best shirt companies in this country would never put a guarantee on their shirts to cover 25 years of hard use and hundreds of washings and ironings.

I continued on, picking up six pairs of wool socks and three pairs of dress socks. I also acquired two ribbed belts, one for work and one for dress. We also received two dress jackets, an overcoat, and a field jacket. Gloves with wool liners were next, as well as a winter helmet liner, which would remind you of a pilot's cap seen in many war movies.

At this point in my trek through the Supply Depot I was starting to get loaded down with clothes. But the Army even covered this problem. I received a duffle bag and proceeded to stuff all of these things into it, wrinkling every piece of clothing that I had just been issued. Before I got out of the Supply Depot, I also received dress shoes, two pairs of boots, linens, and underwear, which again went into that same duffle bag.

After receiving these final items, my duffle bag was completely full and bordered on overflowing. I'm not sure how much all of this stuff weighed, but I can assure you that being a little guy was a definite disadvantage. I ended up dragging my duffle bag through most of the building. Carrying it over my shoulder was a definite impossibility. It had to weigh at least 100 pounds fully loaded. The experts say that most people, if they are in shape, can pick up their own weight and carry it for a while. Now either I was not in shape or the experts on this subject don't have the slightest idea what they are talking about. I knew that I was in good shape for a 22-year-old who had spent the last two years eating pizza, drinking beer, and stuffing down all of the junk food that I could get down in one sitting.

All of this took approximately three hours to accomplish. After exiting the Supply Depot, I walked outside to a bright and sunny crisp February day in the wilds of Kentucky. The way that I was perspiring under the load of the duffle bag combined with the cold that I had acquired overnight put a damper on the otherwise decent winter day that I was experiencing.

Once again, those of us who had finished the process of receiving our issue of clothes had to wait outside for the rest of the trainees to finish. This took another hour or so. I was feeling lousy and try as I may, I could find nothing to be thrilled about at this point in my Army career. By the time we trudged back to our temporary housing and threw our duffle bags on our assigned bunks I thought sure that it was time for lunch. After all, it was 11:45 a.m. and I was getting really hungry.

The Army had different ideas on the subject. Fitness of young men is a big thing. The Army believes, above everything else, that if you are physically fit you can overcome most any obstacle. Keeping this in mind, our next activity for the day was more exercise—just what I needed. My arms and back were killing me already. We were herded outside again and told to strip down to our T-shirts, pants, shoes, and socks. We then proceeded to do exercises for about 30 minutes, which added to my misery. After our midday exercise program was completed, we were then instructed to go change into our newly acquired fatigue clothing and to get ready to march to the Mess Hall for our midday meal. By the time we reached the Mess Hall for lunch, it was after 1:00 p.m.

After another uninspiring meal, we were marched back to our barracks and given the rest of the day to ourselves to unpack our newly acquired clothing, clean up, etc. We were told that getting to the Mess Hall for the evening meal was our responsibility, and that if we needed any personal items we could go to the PX on the Fort and purchase them. However, beer and candy were off limits. Anyone caught with this stuff when we were assigned to our permanent Basic Training Companies later in the week would be dealt with severely. The way I felt at the time, some good cold medicine sounded better. As might be expected, some of the guys didn't take these instructions seriously. You would be amazed at how much beer and candy made its way into our barracks that evening. There were also a lot of guys sicker than a dog the next morning at 0430!

The next couple of days went by quickly as we trainees completed our processing-in. We were herded through the Personnel department, the medical facility, and the local base barbershop for the traditional "skinning-of-the-head ceremony" that the U.S. Armed Services is well-known for in the civilian world. By the end of the first week in the Army, we trainees all looked similar and dressed alike except for our obvious weight and height differences. Non-conformity to the system was totally out of the question.

I personally didn't mind the short-hair look, and with everybody else looking just about as bad as I did, my ego went largely unaffected by this degrading ceremony that the Army takes great pride and satisfaction in accomplishing. You see, part of the military psychology is to first degrade the individual into believing that he is truly a nobody in a group of nobodies and that only as a team does the unit survive in a critical war situation. Individuality plays a very small role in the Army's grand scheme of things. One guy working on his own can mess up things for the whole group.

I realized this many times during my stint in Basic Training. I'll touch on this later in the book, but for now it must be said that in Basic Training nobody did things on his own without paying a painful price to his superiors or receiving the wrath of his Basic Training buddies. I caught on to this system very quickly and although I had very strong thoughts about being able to think as an individual, I knew that this was no place and certainly not the time to express these views.

Something worth mentioning here was our trip to the Fort Campbell Medical and Dental Facility. If you will recall, prior to my formal entrance into the Army I received two complete physicals that both determined that I was in perfect health. Apparently, the boys at Fort Campbell were not informed of this fact. We were all systematically sent through yet another complete medical and dental evaluation during our first few days in the Army. Either the regular Army medical personnel didn't trust the folks in Chicago to do our examinations correctly, or they just wanted to confirm for the third time that we weren't all carriers of the Black Plague.

I amazingly passed my medical and dental examinations for the third time. There was no mention of my heart murmur, my leg problem, or my oncoming cold. I was stuck in this deal and I knew it. This was a hell of a time to be in perfect health!

We spent an entire day in the Personnel section of the Transient Company during that first week. Here we were given intelligence tests, and we talked with various people in regard to where the Army felt we would best fit into the system. After taking the basic tests, which involved basic mathematics, language arts, and so forth, I along with a much smaller group of guys were required to take the Officer's Candidate Test. Your scores coming out of the basic test apparently determined whether you took the Officer's test or not. If your scores were high enough on the first test, the Army made you take the other one.

It must be noted here that several of the guys I was with actually tried to screw these tests up and purposely not do well in hopes that the Army would weed them out on the stupidity factor. There were a lot of stupid guys in this group, but I don't recall losing any of them after the tests were completed. The Army apparently felt that it could make use of just about anyone as long as they had two arms, two legs, one head, and most of their fingers and toes attached.

I took a different approach to this testing than most of the guys did. I was determined to find a niche in the Army where a guy could survive for two years without getting shot at by some clown over in Vietnam. My mama didn't raise no dummy! Only fools wanted to go to Vietnam. I decided that there had to be hundreds of ways to serve your country without having to lie in some rice paddy with bullets zinging over your head. I took these thoughts into the tests, and I ended up doing pretty well. I passed both tests with fairly high scores and even qualified for Officer Candidate School. However, I was told that the school was completely full at the time and no new applications were being taken. I didn't mind. I was only planning a two-year stay in the Army anyway, and officers had to reenlist for a longer stay. There was no way I was going to do that!

CHAPTER FOUR:

Hey You Trainee!

Properly dressed in full military garb, freshly groomed with practically no hair on my head, and given yet another clean bill of health by the Army witch doctors, I was ready as possible to begin my new life in the military. My new title in this truly unique way of life made no reference to my former civilian name. In fact, I was to find out that for the next eight weeks I would have no name. I was simply referred to as "trainee." I acquired several other nicknames during these eight weeks, but we won't mention them just yet.

Several of the guys I met on the first day and I were assigned to a Basic Training Company at the end of the first week. The following Monday we were marched over to our new Company's Bag and Baggage building. It wasn't a long distance to our barracks, but dragging an overstuffed duffle bag and the rest of the stuff that I brought with me from Chicago seemed like an all-day march. That first day was spent mainly going through the formalities of orientation and the assignment of bays, which are large rooms with rows of bunk beds on both sides of the room, allowing for a wide center aisle between the rows of beds. We were given a bunk, shown the bathroom facilities, the dining area, the Orderly Room, etc. We were given the ground rules as to our behavior and what was in store for us over the next eight weeks. This was all discussed at length by a less-than-personable entity that we would come to know as our Drill Instructor.

The real Army training began at 0430 the following morning. Our D.I., whom I will leave nameless for many reasons, gave us our wakeup call at precisely 0430. In true military form, he entered our bay very quietly, flipped on every light in the room at once, and screaming at the top of his lungs told everybody to get their asses out of bed! Once he had assured himself that everyone was sufficiently awake, he then instructed that we had exactly 10 minutes to get dressed in fatigue pants, boots, and T-shirts only, and to get our "swinging dicks" outside and lined up in some kind of orderly formation.

Remember that it was still only the third week of February. Our D.I. made absolutely no mention in his orders about an outer garment. As I stumbled outside along with the others, I realized the fact that not only had the D.I. failed to mention a coat for our attire, but that it was extremely chilly and pitch-black outdoors. I could not for the life of me figure out what we could possibly do at this time of day outside without coats on in the middle of February. After about five minutes out in the cold, we were definitely all awake and ready to do just about anything besides stand around and freeze to death. We had our wish granted. The D.I. came outside in amazingly the same dress as the rest of us and proceeded to tell us that our first move of the day was to run up the road to a streetlight pole and return to the barracks as soon as possible. He was actually going to run with us to see that we not only went the whole distance, but that we ran the whole time.

This little trek lasted about 15 minutes by the time all of the trainees struggled back to the barracks area. Those of us who had gotten back sooner than the rest of the group were required to again stand outside and wait for the rest to return. I figured out right away that there was absolutely no advantage to doing this little run in a hurry. The reward for finishing first was simply a longer wait in the cold. In fact, I found out that the longer you stretched this ordeal out, the warmer you could stay while the others stood around and froze to death. Self-preservation was not one of the early techniques that was taught in the Army, but I decided on this first run that I would include it in the training—whether the Army knew it or not. Besides, at this time of day I was totally incapable of doing anything in a hurry anyway.

I found out later that the actual distance that we ran was approximately a mile- and-a-half. I was amazed that I was still in one piece since I, to my knowledge, had never run this far in one stretch in my whole life. By the time I finished the run everything on and in my body hurt, and breathing was a virtual impossibility. It felt like some big guy had just reached into my chest cavity and was systematically pulling my lungs out through my rib cage. My legs and arms had no feeling at all, and I knew for sure that I had developed blisters on both of my feet. The only good thing that this run had done for me was that my sinuses were now extremely clear.

Another side effect of this little run was that I found myself sick to my stomach and nauseated beyond belief. This feeling was not improved by our next activity, which was physical therapy, or "P.T.," as they called it. What they actually meant was exercise class. This included the usual exercises that most kids do throughout their schooling such as push-ups, sit-ups, running in place, jumping jacks, and burpies. (A burpy is an exercise in which you drop down from a standing position to a push-up position, and then you push yourself back up to a position where your knees are bent. Then you jump from there back up to a standing position, all in a fluid non-stop motion.) This lasted another 15 minutes or so. By the time we had finished this activity, only the guys in the best shape were left standing on the front lawn of the barracks area. Like most of the guys in my training group, I was dying on the front lawn of the barracks area.

It was now approximately 0500 and still very dark outside. Our D.I. spent the next 15 minutes berating us on our seemingly lack of physical conditioning. He went on to say that before we were through with our Basic Training under his masterful teaching we would be in the best shape of our entire lives. Standing there holding my side and struggling to breathe in a normal fashion, I wanted to disagree with him but I couldn't even utter a weak groan. I'm sure this was the whole idea.

We were given about five minutes to regain our energy and breath. We were then marched over to the Mess Hall for another exciting breakfast. As sick as I was after all of this activity so early in the day, the thought of eating was repulsive. I managed to force down a few bites of powdered eggs and toast, fighting nausea all the way. I was also sure that the cold I had been fighting off for a week now was firmly in place and would be with me for some time. Being chilled and shivering was becoming the norm in this new life.

What we went through during the first two weeks of our Basic Training was primarily designed to get us into the shape that our D.I. described to us that first morning. We did a lot of running, exercise, and marching. The Army did use some common sense though when we practiced our marching and parading. They let us wear our field jackets and caps. The D.I. explained why they let us wear the jackets for this activity and not the other two activities. He told us that running and exercise have a tendency to overheat the body. Therefore, jackets were not necessary even in cold weather to keep warm for short periods of time. Marching, on the other hand, was a more subdued activity than running, and therefore the jackets were necessary. Everything in the Army was determined by its necessity for survival. He pointed out that if we were running in an attack on the enemy in the Arctic Circle, the last thing that we would be concerned with was how cold it was outside.

We received a lot of these explanations throughout our training in these first few weeks. What scared me as I went along with all of this was that these explanations started to make sense. After all, we were in the Army for one reason—to learn how to be combat soldiers. Survival in combat conditions was an absolute necessity for success of the mission. You can't win battles and wars when your men are lying on the ground suffering from heat and exhaustion. They must all be in excellent shape and be able to survive under the worst conditions imaginable. But instead of feeling like I was in good shape, I felt the worst that I could remember since I had the flu when I was a kid. In fact, I wasn't so sure that I didn't have the flu.

This thought brings up another event that I will always remember about my Basic Training in the U.S. Army. The event that I am about to describe had long-lasting effects on my training. It eventually caused this training to last 12 weeks instead of the typical eight weeks. It also, as it turned out, changed everything that was to happen to me over the next two years of my life. In some respects, it turned out OK, and in others it turned out absolutely lousy. As I continue this story I think you will see what I mean. The only consolation that I received from this was that I was one of many to be involved in the event since there is nothing worse than being alone. At least with numbers you get a false sense of security that everything will turn out OK no matter how bad things get or seem. The following description will also give you a prime example of the military psychology and methodology in its finest form.

CHAPTER FIVE:

The Great Blizzard

About two weeks into my Basic Training, there was a major winter storm in the wilds of Kentucky. High winds fueled a six- to eight-inch snowfall into a major blizzard. Fortunately for our training, it occurred over the weekend. By the following Monday the weather had cleared enough not to stop anything.

Now there is nothing unusual about snow in Kentucky in February. However, the Army had an interesting program in place to combat winter boredom on the weekends by confining 30 guys in a large bay in the barracks. You see, we were confined to our barracks on the weekends so that we couldn't get into any trouble on the Post. We could do what we wanted to as long as we didn't leave the Company grounds. Isolation was another form of Army discipline. After all, as trainees we were next to sub-human in the military and until we received enough training from our brilliant D.I., we could not be allowed to associate with the rest of the military world.

The program that I'm referring to was that in each bay at night every window had to be open a minimum of six inches to ensure enough fresh air for everyone. It is a well-known fact that the Army takes in many kinds of folks from a lot of different areas. Simple things like bathing regularly, washing your hands before meals, brushing your teeth, and the like are not always the norm for everyone in the group. So to hold down the possibility of disease and sickness, fresh air was the only way to go in the military. Not really a bad idea! However, in February it is fairly cold at night and it consistently gets down in the teens in Kentucky.

You can just imagine what the temperature was in our bay with every window in the room open not less than six inches. It definitely cut down the possibility of foul odors. Whether it did any other good, I question vehemently. The worst part of this was like many other procedures in the Army, there was no room for discussion on whether we thought it was a good idea or not. This was an order, not a suggested policy. We trainees were in no position to question any policy put in place by our instructors. Therefore, every night we slept in a cold room with nothing but a single Army blanket and a sheet to cover ourselves with. This may seem healthy to some people, but I thought it was crazy as hell! I was willing to take my chances with body odor.

Well, like many other things in this new life that I was leading, I even started getting used to this idea. I still thought it was crazy, but who was I to question a system that had been in place long before I got involved with it? My cold wasn't getting any better, but spring would be here in a couple of months and the nights were bound to get warmer by the end of my training. This rationalization of my situation did a respectable job of covering this open-window policy—until the weekend of the "Great Blizzard."

It had begun snowing and blowing that Saturday afternoon. By Saturday evening the conditions outside were harsh enough to convince even the stupidest soul that outside was strictly off-limits for human survival. In spite of the external conditions, our bay had remained relatively comfortable all day mainly because no one had been stupid enough to open the windows. However, as rack time closed in a member of the Company cadre came by as usual to see that we were complying with the open-window policy. Of course, he saw that none of the windows were open. Several of us tried to explain to him that we thought since it was so bad outside that the open-window policy was not a good idea for this one night. He didn't agree, and the windows were opened.

Rather than spend any more time in the bay than was necessary, I decided that it was a good time to take a hot shower. I stayed in the shower as long as I could but there were some other guys with the same idea, and sharing a shower was not my idea of fun. As I came out of the bathroom, which was down the hall from the bay, I noticed that there was quite a breeze in the hallway. As I approached the double doors to the bay I also saw the strangest sight that I have ever seen inside of a building. I couldn't believe it. There was actually snow blowing from one side of our bay to the other side through all of the open windows! At this point I couldn't stand it anymore. At the risk of looking stupid and taking a chance on receiving major verbal abuse from the D.I. on duty that weekend, I decided that somebody had to do something about this nonsense.

Wrapped in only a towel, I walked down to the D.I.'s quarters and knocked on the door. As I knocked on his door, my only hope was that the wind outside would keep blowing long enough to get him to come down to the bay and see the snow flying around. If the wind were to suddenly stop I would have a miserable time bothering him on a Saturday night. Bravery in the face of intimidation was never one of my strong suits. And believe me, bothering a D.I. over Army policy that you didn't agree with was the height of intimidation. I had already seen in the first two weeks of Basic Training that disagreeing with a D.I. on anything was bad business, even if you were right.

I was just sick enough with chills that I decided to take the risk anyway. As it turned out, he came down to the bay and actually agreed that the windows needed to be shut. He also noticed that I didn't look too great. In fact, neither did nearly three-quarters of the guys in our bay. We were all coughing and suffering with chills and fever. About an hour later, an Army medical officer showed up at our barracks and began taking everyone's temperature. Mine read 102 degrees, and I was instructed to get dressed and get ready to go to the Infirmary. That night, the Fort Campbell Hospital admitted nearly two-thirds of our Company with upper respiratory infections. We all had temperatures ranging from slightly above 99 degrees to 104 degrees.

I wasn't sure what exactly an upper respiratory infection was. All I knew was that I was sicker than a dog the night I was admitted to the hospital. Everything it seemed that could ache ached. I was coughing on a regular basis and my head felt like it was on fire. I did find out one good thing about being in the hospital though—all of the windows were closed. They must have not been informed that it was Army policy to have the windows open where trainees were housed. But of course I never asked about it.

I spent approximately six days in the hospital recovering from this unknown disease. I was given hardly any medication that I know of, but I was told to drink loads of water and Kool-Aid on what seemed like a 24-hour schedule. They checked my temperature three times a day, and then simply told me to keep drinking fluids as much as I could. My temperature returned to normal very slowly, and the only benefit that I could see from doing all of this drinking was that my kidneys got a good workout.

After about four days of steady drinking and very little sleep, a doctor came by to check me out. My temperature was down to about 99 degrees and I was feeling slightly better than I was my first night in the hospital. His only comment to me was that he thought I wasn't drinking enough. That was why I wasn't well enough to leave, and he insisted that I increase my fluid intake. Since I was already floating an arc in the ocean this idea of his really astounded me. I naturally got a little ticked at his suggestion that it was my own fault that my temperature had not returned to normal. I told him that if he would give me a shot of penicillin or even a couple of aspirin that I would get out of his hair as soon as possible. At this remark, he reminded me that he was the doctor and he told me to keep drinking.

By the sixth day my health was restored well enough for them to release me to Active Duty. My nose was still running and some symptoms of the original cold I had were still around, but I felt reasonably well enough to do something besides lay in a hospital bed and drink Kool-Aid all day. Upon my return to the Company after missing nearly a full week of training was when I received my first major disappointment of my Army career. I was informed that since I had missed the third week of training that I was going to be recycled to another Company that was just beginning its training. It was felt that missing a full week of training was too much to make up in the four weeks that were left. The guys who had managed to stay out of the hospital had already gone to the rifle range and were into full-fledged combat training by this time.

I was going to have to go back to the first week of training again and start all over. I just couldn't wait! I had a one-word expression for this—"SHIT!" But I wasn't alone. Several other guys received the same good news. The following Monday I found myself walking over to my new Company dragging my overstuffed duffle bag with me.

CHAPTER SIX:

Recycled Misfits

As I walked into the parking lot of my new Company, I was trying to find something good about starting my training all over again but try as I may, I could not find a single thing to be happy about. I was not looking forward to all of the initial harassment that is usually given to new recruits in Basic Training. I had already gone through two weeks of this and felt that I didn't need any more attitude adjustments. In fact, I almost considered myself a veteran of sorts. I had been in the Army nearly three weeks longer than the guys I was about to join.

My first encounter with one of the D.I.'s with this new Company didn't do anything to improve my spirits. I was lugging my duffle bag around every place I went. Suddenly an absolutely brilliant idea came into my head: Why not leave my stuff outside while I went into the Orderly Room to process into this new Company? It would save having to carry it any more than I needed to. I left it leaning against the bumper of a car in the parking lot until I finished finding out where I was supposed to go and so forth. This turned out to be a major mistake. When I came back out to retrieve my stuff I found a little guy not much bigger than me standing near the car glaring at my duffle bag. This is when I found out that this car belonged to one of my new D.I.'s, and he didn't like stuff leaning against it.

Naturally, I instantaneously endeared myself to this guy for the rest of my eight weeks of training. To put it mildly, he hated my ass and never let me forget the mistake I had made. Every chance he got he did everything he could to make my life miserable. Me being basically a nice guy did the same for him. You see, I was a real shithead when I was a kid and I often got away with murder on a regular basis. I was always small and received more than my share of attention because of it. I learned at an early age that you can get a lot further with manipulation of the mind than by using brute force with people. I knew that for this guy I was going to have to figure out a way to either avoid him altogether for the next eight weeks or work around him.

The chances of avoiding him looked slim at best, so I opted for the latter idea. As soon as I could I started pleasing my regular Platoon D.I. and made myself useful to him. Having already gone through the first two weeks of training worked to my advantage. I naturally appeared brighter than the others because many times I already knew what to do in the drills. He made me a Platoon leader right out of the chute. A Platoon leader was simply one of the guys in the Platoon named by the D.I. based on who he felt could help the others best and lead them in his absence. This guy also acted as the spokesman for the Platoon if there were any problems that needed to be resolved. It was a temporary promotion of sorts without an official rank.

The D.I. apparently also found out that I was a college graduate early in our training. There were three of us in this new Platoon who had been to college prior to being drafted. As it turned out, all three of us became Platoon leaders. I could see that our D.I. was no slouch and that he was going to make his work as easy as possible. We were immediately put in charge of seeing that everyone in the Platoon passed all of the exams that we were required to take with flying colors, among other extraneous duties.

There were several D.I.'s, depending on the activity we were doing at the time. They each had an area of instruction assigned to them, and often they would trade off assignments depending on their assigned days off. However, one of them was our main D.I. that we actually answered to and asked questions of.

My new Company was made up of guys who had been recycled like myself from other Companies that were in training at the time at Fort Campbell. It didn't take long, however, to find out that all of these guys were not recycled for the same reasons. Some had arrived because of disciplinary reasons or because they just couldn't keep up with the training in their previous Company. I realized that I was in a large group of misfits and that we were in one of the toughest training units on the Post. This was going to be a really interesting eight weeks.

There were many things that happened during this time that I could relate to you because nearly every day something funny or strange took place. I'll try not to bore you with too many stories. To begin with, here is a description of our D.I., a character in his own right. Again, I will leave him nameless simply because all of the D.I.'s that I ran into in the Army fit a similar mold—they were all fanatics! Ours was no exception. One day he could be funny and we had a great time in our training, and the next day he could be a real asshole and make everybody shit bricks all day. He was a real-life Dr. Jekyll and Mr. Hyde. He was arrogant, and he loved to show off his abilities at hand-to-hand combat. He also got a big charge out of embarrassing people. He was in excellent shape and he convinced everyone in the Platoon that on any given day, he could whip any one of us in short order.

The guy was 24 years old and a Vietnam veteran, and he drove a brand-new Ford Mustang Mach I. He was quite a lady's man, or at least he thought he was. He also drove like a maniac. He used to show up late once in a while for our early formations and you could hear him coming from a mile away. How he managed to keep from wrecking his car over the eight weeks that I knew him was beyond me. He didn't treat Army trucks any better than his car. He drove the hell out of them as well, and it made no difference to him whether he was carrying passengers or not. We all survived our trips to the rifle range and the like in spite of his driving. I sometimes thought that he was disappointed by this. This guy was a southerner all the way. Fortunately, he never held it against me that I was from Chicago. He was determined from the start of our training to whip us all into a close-knit, top-of-the-line Basic Training Unit. This presented quite a challenge considering some of the guys who were in our Platoon.

His first move to ensure that we all knew where our loyalties belonged was to hang a rebel flag at one end of our bay area. He made it very clear that we were going to be the best Platoon in the Company no matter what it took. He was not going to be second-best at anything, and neither were we. He was going to see to this come hell or high water. He also stated many times that anyone who disagreed with this idea was going to shape up and become convinced to agree with him.

As might be expected, a few jerks questioned his authority and his ideas over the eight weeks of training. Believe me, it was not a pretty sight to watch people receive attitude adjustments. Quite often the adjustments took place in front of the whole Platoon. Don't get me wrong though. I never personally saw any D.I. lay a hand on anybody. Psychological and verbal abuse combined with sheer embarrassment often did a very effective job. There were things that were done that I disagreed with and saw no purpose for though.

For example, we were in formation one morning as was the normal routine every morning before we began each day's activities. One of the purposes of this formation was to of course see if everyone was still around. And yes, one morning some people were missing but that's another story in itself. Another purpose of the formation was to see if everybody was properly clad and groomed to Army specifications. This included shaving every day without fail. Now shaving for me was no big deal. I had been shaving regularly since I was about 15. However, for others in the group shaving was practically unheard of in their daily lives. The majority of the guys that I was with in the Army were barely out of high school.

D.I.'s were very consistent in one respect—they all believed in Army policy to the letter. How they chose to implement it was a whole new ball game. I'm sure that the Army had certain guidelines for the D.I.'s to follow in our training. After all, they had guidelines for everything. However, it sometimes seemed that the D.I.'s strayed beyond the guidelines and went strictly at their own whim—freelancing so to speak.

As I mentioned earlier, our D.I. was kind of a Dr. Jekyll and Mr. Hyde. This particular morning he was definitely Mr. Hyde. We had an 18-year-old kid in our Platoon from the mountains of Tennessee. He was very shy and introverted. When he did talk to anybody, he talked very fast and was barely understandable. He had a strong southern accent besides everything else. What came out of his mouth often sounded garbled. The kid was scared shitless of the D.I., and the D.I. knew it. The poor kid couldn't do anything right. He couldn't march or even stay in step with anybody. He was a total wimp at hand-to-hand combat, and push-ups and sit-ups were impossible for him.

As might be expected, this kid became our D.I.'s whipping boy very early in the training. What made things worse for the kid was that before he was drafted into the Army I don't believe that he had ever shaved a day in his life. He had nothing to shave! He had a few stray hairs of peach fuzz, but that was it. In the mornings he spent more time repairing the damage he had done to himself with the razor than he did actually shaving. Needless to say, his face was raw from shaving most of the time. Well, it got so bad that he finally just quit shaving altogether in fear of doing permanent damage.

As Mr. Hyde checked us all out on that particular morning, he came over to this kid. Noticing that the kid had obviously not shaved, he went completely into orbit. He yanked the kid out of formation, got right in his face, and screamed at the top of his lungs for at least two minutes about not shaving. He called this kid every name in the book, and then a few more. He then made the kid go inside the barracks, get his razor, and come back outside. He then proceeded to order this kid to dry-shave in front of all of us. While the kid dry-shaved his face, Mr. Hyde then calmly made sure that the rest of us understood the Army policy on shaving every day. Amazingly, there were a couple of jerks in the fourth row of the formation who found humor in all of this. They spent the whole session snickering under their breath. When Mr. Hyde got through with them they had joined "whipping boy" in dry-shaving. It wasn't nearly as funny at this point.

To say the least, the rest of us got the message right off the bat. Now this sort of treatment really bordered on sheer harassment in my opinion. I must admit though that it was very effective in its results. I must tell you that the trainees involved in this incident did survive this treatment with no long-lasting scars or anything. And after that morning, there was always a mad rush for the bathroom to shave before any of our formations.

In spite of all the harassment and belittling acts that many of us were subjected to, Basic Training in the Army was not all that dreary. There were many things that happened during those eight, or in my case 12 weeks, that were really quite hilarious. The training was tough and the days were long, but there were many humorous moments and events that I will always remember.

Being appointed a Platoon leader was not always the greatest position to be in. Quite often, the D.I.'s used us as guinea pigs for their many demonstrations. They would, for example, pit you against some guy twice your size to demonstrate some form of hand-to-hand combat. There were many times I ended up on the ground with pain all over my body. All you could do at this point was to get back up and grin and bear it to save face. I'm not sure, but I think the D.I.'s got some kind of perverted pleasure out of all of this. We were also expected to do better than the others in the Platoon on the tests and in the endurance races. If the D.I.'s thought you were loafing through any of this they would get on your case even more because you were a Platoon leader. You were expected to be better than the other guys. I definitely got my share of abuse.

One of my favorite parts of the training was the hand-to-hand combat, especially when they provided us with rifles. We had to learn various attack and defense maneuvers using our rifles as weapons. The approach in all of this was that you had to assume you had just run out of ammunition and you were engaged in fierce one-on-one combat with a crazed Communist insurgent who was bent on knocking your fool head off. And of course you were supposed to be thinking the same way—kill or be killed! One of the keys to all of this hand-to-hand combat was how loud you could yell some blood-curdling expletive about the other guy's mother. The theory behind this, according to the D.I., was that if you were screaming in this manner it would throw off your opponent's timing just long enough to give you the advantage in the combat.

Apparently, this tactic has been used for many centuries as an effective combat technique. They told us that the Vietcong, who were organized insurgents backed and supplied by the North Vietnam Communist Government, did this stuff all the time when they attacked our Posts in Vietnam. Well, having a good set of lungs and a very large vocabulary, I handled this technique extremely well. I was by far one of the best yellers in the Platoon. It was difficult, however, to take all of this seriously when you were engaged in combat with one of your fellow trainees.

We spent a great majority of the sessions yelling stupid things to each other just to get your opponent to laugh. The D.I.'s tried to maintain some kind of professional order to all of this, but they often fell into fits of laughter along with the rest of us at some of the stupid things people yelled. How effective we all ended up in this sort of thing was truly questionable. I remember one guy asking the D.I. during one of these sessions to explain why all of the yelling was necessary. The D.I. replied that just in case you weren't any good at the combat techniques, you would still have the possibility of defeating the enemy by scaring him to death.

This I never bought! I could just see myself screaming at some little dude hoping to scare him to death while he was systematically lopping off my arms with a bayonet that he had been honing for sharpness over the past month. I did think that the yelling would be useful in one respect though. If you were running for your life away from this crazy enemy it would be extremely beneficial to yell for help. It would also identify you as the chicken American so that your own guys wouldn't mistake you for the enemy and blow your shit away. As you can see, I had very little faith in my hand-to-hand combat abilities. If I was in the situation where I had just run out of ammunition, I would be hoping that the Army either would get me the hell out of that situation or send in the cavalry. That's the way all the war movies went that I had watched anyway.

I did have one day of glory, however. We were attacking automobile tires stuffed with straw with rubber heads attached to them. I had been having a rough time with this training for about a week. No matter how hard I tried, I just wasn't very effective at killing the enemy on a direct charge with bayonets. We were supposed to charge the dummies, thrust our bayonets into their midsections, pull back out, and give them a butt stroke to the head. We went through a series of these acting like we were over-running an enemy encampment, killing several of the defenders as we went. My problem was that after stabbing the first guy I could never get my bayonet back out of his midsection. Or I would miss it altogether and fall flat on my face. The D.I. was on me all the time and kept yelling at me that I was dead already.

I finally made up my mind that I was going to do it right and get the D.I. off my case. My turn for the charge came. I went running toward the first dummy screaming like a wild man, stabbed the guy, and proceeded to hit the dummy's head so hard that it flew off the tire and landed about 20 feet away. I then went through the rest of the tires with the same tenacity, and I ended up supposedly over-running the camp single-handedly. Needless to say, I impressed not only the D.I. but the rest of the guys in the Platoon.

I had finally arrived! I was a deadly part of the U.S. War Machine. I was invincible! I immediately adopted the following motto: "Yeah though I walk through the valley of the shadow of death, I will fear no evil because I'm the meanest son of a bitch in the valley!" Well, not quite. But I was close to it. My reward for all of this unnatural behavior was a one-inch gash on my hand that was caused by the safety switch on my rifle when I stabbed the first dummy. I refused to show it, but the pain that I was feeling in my hand made me question who had gotten the worse end of my attack—the dummies or me. In any case, I had finally passed this portion of my training.

The rifle range also gave me a lot of fits. As you will recall, I mentioned that before entering the Army I had never shot a gun. Well as might be expected, I was definitely a rookie at the rifle range. When we first started I couldn't hit the broad side of a barn. I wrote all of this off as simply a lack of experience. However, it became apparent as the training went along that this was not going to be one of my better areas. I am naturally right-handed, so it was logical to learn to shoot right-handed. But I had a little problem with this. I couldn't for the life of me get my M-16 adjusted the right way so that I could put three shots under a quarter on a target that was only 25 feet away. This was critical to the whole scheme of things. If your M-16 wasn't zeroed-in you couldn't go on with the training.

I spent two days shooting right-handed, wasting 48 rounds of ammunition. And I still never got anything closer together on a target than about an inch apart. My buddy—the D.I.—the one that I had pissed off when I first came to the Company was the guy running the rifle range. I was clearly irritating this guy to no end. By the time I had gone through the 48 rounds, he was a stark-raving maniac. He finally told me to turn around and try it left-handed once. My first three shots were under a quarter on the target. Now you would think that the guy would be happy that I had accomplished this, but not this guy. He whacked me over the helmet with his baton and screamed at me for a full minute accusing me of being left-handed all along and not telling him. I tried to convince him that I was really right-handed, but I might as well have been trying to sell him some good swampland in Arizona. He refused to believe anything I said. He was so disgusted with me that after he ran out of things to call me he just sent me on to the next station without any further instruction. And he was still fuming at the end of the day.

I spent the rest of my Army career shooting left-handed, and I even managed to get fairly proficient at it. I was to find out much later when I was in Korea that the problem with my shooting was that I needed glasses. This was to correct a double-vision problem that I had had for years due to a lazy right eye. In any case, I adapted to left-handed shooting and had no further problems at the rifle range. In fact, I ended up getting a Sharpshooter rating out of Basic Training, which I didn't think was too bad considering.

Marching was an everyday occurrence all the way through Basic Training. I have never fully understood why the Army places so much emphasis on this particular phase of the training. We used to drill for what seemed like hours on end. It had to do with discipline I guess. I guess they figured that if you could follow directions in a marching drill and not question a thing, then you could do the same in a battle situation. It may have to do with simple organization. It definitely stressed togetherness. If one guy goofed up, everybody paid for his mistake. I can still recall the hundreds of push-ups that we had to do while we were all learning to march correctly. This activity was the reason for an awful lot of the highlights and funnier moments that I experienced while I was in the Army.

We had two guys in our Platoon who I believe never did learn how to march correctly. What made these two guys even more entertaining was that their names were similar and they came from the same area of the country. Our D.I. could never keep their names straight and since they both had the same problem, he was constantly yelling at one or both of them. He got so frustrated with the fact that he couldn't get them in step or to follow his directions correctly that he finally made them road guards on each side of the formations. Road guards were the guys who couldn't do anything right while they were marching. They were put out to the sides of the formation so they didn't mess everybody else up. To solve the problem with their names, our D.I. finally just started calling them "One" and "Two." It was simpler than trying to remember their names and which one was which.

We all got a lot of laughs out of marching. It was just like so many movies I had seen with the Three Stooges, Laurel and Hardy, and Abbott and Costello. You know, where the D.I. yells, "Left face" and everybody goes right face. Or we'd be marching in one direction and he'd yell "To the rear march," and at least one guy would keep going the same way while the rest of the group turned around and went the other way. I never would have believed that this could happen in real life. I always thought that it was a staged thing for the movies. This happened so often during the first few weeks that it just got funnier and funnier and the D.I. got angrier and angrier. But like everything else, after a while our little band of misfits learned to march, and we even won the award for drill at our graduation ceremony.

I mentioned earlier that our Platoon had some real characters in it, and our D.I. was just one of them. We had the bullies, the comedians, the jerks, and the nerds, and we even had a momma's boy or two. We were from all walks of life and from every part of the country. We had college graduates, as well as guys who had only a grade-school education. We had guys from very well-to-do and affluent families, and those who had come from the poorest backgrounds imaginable. Somehow or another through the miracle of togetherness, we amazingly all got along fairly well and actually got to a point where we worked together as a close and cohesive unit. We helped each other to overcome individual weaknesses and we became friends, at least for a short time.

We all did our share of growing up and out in Basic Training. Maturity in men comes slowly sometimes. It has often been said that this is one thing that the Army does for you. I'm not sure that it makes you more mature or even a man, but the experience of interacting with other people definitely makes you more aware of the world around you and how short life really is. Life in the barracks with 25 or 30 other guys had its good points and its bad points. On the one hand, there was never any loneliness. I can't remember a single time when at least somebody wasn't around to talk to when you needed it. We all were pretty much in the same position. We were isolated from the real world. It wasn't until very late in the training that the Army felt we were brainwashed enough to let us loose in the outside world.

The last few weekends of the training were left pretty much to our own devices for entertainment. They even let us off the Post. The only rules were that we had to be back by the following Monday morning for formation. A few others and I did get into Hopkinsville, Kentucky, which was a couple of miles down the road from the Fort, once or twice for a few beers and the like. I must tell you that after spending that much time with 25 or 30 guys, any diversion in the real world was better than sitting around in the barracks reading or playing cards. After all, the real world had girls! Even the ugly ones began to look good after a few beers.

Being one of the older guys in the group, I had much better control and was very sensible along these lines. Some of these kids had absolutely no control over their biological functions and pursued practically anything that wiggled. I guess it was the last fling that I had in college that cooled my passions for the opposite sex. I had been sour on relationships with girls ever since I had broken up with my one college flame. You see, up to this point in my life I had not had that many serious feelings about girls. Oh, I had my share of dates when I was a kid in high school and I felt that I had been in love a couple of times by the time I graduated from college. However, none of these experiences had really grown into any long-term commitments. In fact, I was fairly naive for a long time on the laws of nature and how to interact with women.

In any case, when my last fling had fallen apart with the return of her old boyfriend from Vietnam, I was definitely down on women and wasn't seriously looking to begin any new relationships at the time. I was tired of chasing after them and tired of getting hurt. I had decided that the next time I fell in love with a girl that it was going to be a permanent relationship. I was only 22 years old, and there was plenty of time to find the right girl and settle down. Besides, ever since I had been drafted into the Army there was no guarantee that I was even going to survive this experience. Guys were dying in the jungles and in rice paddies in Vietnam every day, and there was no assurance that all of us weren't going to end up there ourselves.

This was a real possibility in the spring of 1971. By this time, our government was fully committed to a strong involvement in the Vietnam Police Action. Half-a- million troops had turned this little Police Action into an all-out war, and the need for more men to replace those who had already died was an ever-pressing reality. You could just sense it in the manner in which we were being trained. There was a strong emphasis on survival, and there was a deep sense of urgency in the eyes and voices of our D.I.'s. They knew what all of this was about. Some of them had already been in Vietnam and knew what we all might be headed for in the very near future. This was serious shit! We were being trained to kill people—this wasn't a Boy Scout outing! The younger guys probably didn't think about all of this stuff. They were too busy growing up, and for many of them they were enjoying their first experience of being out in the world on their own. I had the feeling that some of these guys wouldn't make it to their 22nd birthdays. A morbid thought to say the least, but it was reality whether we liked it or not.

I must relate a couple more incidents that happened during those eight weeks that reflected the growing anxiety and tension that all of us began to feel as the training continued. They served as comic relief for an otherwise very serious atmosphere that began to develop as our initial training was coming to a close. We had a guy in the Platoon who had the worst body odor problem that I can ever recall. The main problem was that he just didn't do a very good job of keeping clean on a regular basis. He very rarely took a shower, and I don't recall ever seeing him brushing his teeth. His hair was greasy-looking and his hands were nothing short of filthy. I mean, this guy was a real slob! I don't know where he grew up, but whoever supervised his adolescence left several things out of his training. To make things worse, he was a real wimp. Everybody hassled this kid.

Now men have never been known for their concern for staying clean and maintaining a germ-free environment, especially when 25 or 30 of them are together for any length of time. However, in the case of the "No-Wash-Boy," several of us got together one evening and decided that things had gone a little too far this time. This kid was really starting to smell ripe! We came up with several plans as to how to combat this situation. After much laughter and many devious ideas were thrown out, it was decided that a couple of us would lure this kid into the bathroom and then the rest of us would assist him in the ways of how to take an effective shower.

The kid fell for the trap, and once he was in the bathroom the group easily overcame his resistance. He was pushed into the showers that were coincidentally on already, and the "Clean Air Society" completed its mission. The shower that the kid took was truly unique—after all, how many times do you get to take a shower when you have a choice of 10 different kinds of soap to use? The kid obviously did not enjoy his shower. However, he did learn that he should start taking one every so often.

Another morning comes to mind that also gives you a good picture of the conditions of our barracks at the time. The usual routine every morning except on weekends was the following: Our D.I. would casually come into our bay, flip on the lights, and yell at the top of his lungs for everybody to get their swinging dicks out of the rack. And yes, he did use this terminology. Well as you might guess, we all actually got used to this routine after a few weeks. It became so commonplace that there were a couple of guys who could actually sleep through the wake-up call. Usually somebody had to go over and shake these guys out of their slumber. This got to be a real pain after a while. It was hard enough just getting your own systems moving.

On this particular morning, one guy was left alone sawing the sequoias. Nobody bothered to see that he woke up. We all went about our business and quietly left the barracks for our morning formation. The guy was obviously missed in the formation. We all pretty much felt that we had saved him long enough and it was time for him to learn how to fend for himself. Brotherly love has its limits. After the roll call was taken and it was established that this kid was not AWOL but simply still asleep in the barracks, the fun began. The D.I. led us back into the barracks and we very quietly filed back into the bay to witness how to effectively wake up your buddy in three easy steps.

Our D.I. was in his finest form that morning. We had an aisle between the rows of bunks that was kept spotless and shining at all times. It was one of our weekly duties to wash, polish, and buff this aisle to a high glow of sheen. No one was allowed in this aisle at any time. Our D.I. was so fanatical about this aisle being kept to a highly buffed condition that we had even polished this floor on our hands and knees with high-gloss car polish for the past several weeks. As we all stood there in complete shock, our D.I. walked right down the middle of this aisle until he had reached this guy's bunk. Unfortunately for this kid, his bunk was on top. Dr. Jekyll immediately turned into Mr. Hyde. Without saying a word, he grabbed both ends of the mattress that the kid was lying on and removed mattress and kid both from the springs of his bunk. Mattress, covers, and kid ended up out in the middle of the untouchable middle aisle. To say the least, the kid woke up instantly. The embarrassment of the situation definitely made its impression on him. To ensure that he fully understood that getting up every morning was strictly his own responsibility, the D.I. ordered him to spend the rest of the day hand-washing and polishing the floor in our bay. It was not a small floor either. You can just imagine how large a room would have to be to house 25 to 30 guys.

The D.I. also used this opportunity to give us all a lesson in combat training. He calmly pointed out that in a combat situation if this kid continued to sleep so soundly he would be dead in less than five minutes in the event of an enemy attack on this Fort. He pointed out that in sneak attacks by the enemy they don't bother to wake everybody up before they slit your throats. I don't know about everybody else, but I definitely made a mental note of this statement. And to be honest with you, to this day I do not sleep very soundly. This was just one of many experiences during those two years in the Army that changed my life forever.

After nearly 12 weeks of training, graduation day finely arrived. I was extremely proud of myself for surviving Boot Camp. I would say conservatively that I was in excellent shape. I could do things that I had never been able to do before in my life. I was reasonably adept in my skills of hand-to-hand combat, and I could shoot an M-16 rifle—even left-handed—with amazing accuracy. I could run a mile in combat boots with ease and without being out of breath. My best time in this event was 5 minutes, 50 seconds. I wasn't a gazelle by any stretch of the imagination, but I was quick enough to earn the maximum score. Any runner or jogger will tell you that this is not an easy thing to accomplish, especially in combat boots and fatigue pants. I was one mean and lean fighting machine! I was scared of practically no one, and I felt that I could defend myself in a fight with much more assurance of survival than I had ever felt in my whole life.

I never had been a fighter as a kid. I wasn't a wimp or anything, but in the same respect I didn't go around looking for fights either. I had earned my Private's stripe in Basic Training, which didn't always happen. This promotion to the new name of "Private" sure sounded better than "trainee." I had finally become an entity in the U.S. Army. I was no longer considered sub-human. This does wonders for your ego, by the way. I remember calling my brother back in Illinois. When he asked me how things were going, I told him that when I saw him again he had better not mess with me anymore. I now knew several ways to kill him or at least to inflict severe pain on him. He laughed, but I wasn't really kidding around. I would never intentionally hurt anyone, but I was reasonably sure that if necessary I could sure surprise a few people with my hidden violent nature. Being mouthy was one thing. Backing up what you said was another. For the first time in my life, I felt fairly confident of my own abilities in this less-than-honorable expertise.

I still believe that avoiding fights is the only way to go, however. Fighting proves nothing other than the fact that one person can kick the shit out of someone else. It certainly doesn't affect anyone's state of mind. If anything, it polarizes a person's thinking. If someone dislikes you and you beat him to a pulp, he will certainly dislike you more than he did before. As a result, I still haven't ever gotten into a serious fight.

Following graduation with all of its pomp and circumstance that is common in the Army tradition, we all began receiving our orders for our Advanced Training. This is yet another story in my Army experience. As you'll recall, early in our training they had given us all sorts of tests to determine where we would best fit into the Army based on our mental capabilities and our known skills. I had been reasonably sure that my degree in journalism would not be overlooked when it came time to assign me to Advanced Training. I had assumed wrongly, as it turned out, that the Army would have sense enough to see that I would be of much more value to them as a clerk or something in an administrative type of job than as a run-of-the-mill infantryman.

The Army and all of its brilliant bureaucracy did its best to see that I lost complete faith in human common sense. My original orders for Advanced Training were to go to Fort Lee, Virginia and attend Public Information School. This would have been a natural choice considering my schooling and background. Promotions, I'm sure, would have come easily, and there was a very good possibility that I might have gotten away with never leaving the United States during my stay in the Army. I felt that having a college degree in the very field that I would have gone to school for would have worked to my full advantage. They probably would have made me an instructor right out of training. It was commonly known that this sort of thing happened quite often in the Army. They use talent when they see it.

However, my being recycled in Basic Training changed everything. My original orders were flagged, and I had to wait an additional week while the Army's Personnel office came up with new orders for me. Apparently, when your original orders were cancelled due to one reason or another in Basic Training, the Army took those people and put them into a pool of personnel of sorts. Then this pool was used to help fill out rosters for schools that didn't have enough people signed up. I fell fortunately or unfortunately, depending on how you look at it, into this category.

After another endless week in Basic Training, I finally received my new orders. I was called into the Company Commander's office to receive the good news. I was informed that I had been given a Primary MOS (Military Occupational Status) of 16D10, and I was assigned for the next phase of my training at the Air Defense School in Fort Bliss, Texas. To put it mildly, I just couldn't believe it. Here I was the perfect candidate for a Public Information Officer, and these idiots were going to try to turn me into a Missile Launcher Crewman in the high-tech field of air defense! I knew absolutely nothing about missiles.

In my mind, they were out of theirs! I protested to the Company Commander that they had surely made a mistake and had gotten my orders mixed up with someone else's. He assured me that there was no mistake in the orders and thought I should be thrilled and honored with being selected for Air Defense School. To say the least, I was less than enthusiastic about my prospects. Besides, where in the hell was Fort Bliss, Texas? He assured me that I would like it there since it was just outside of El Paso, Texas next to the Mexican border. Oh thrill! Oh thrill! I was going to the desert in the badlands of Texas during the hottest time of the year in June and July. I just couldn't wait for the adventure to begin.

I was given a week of leave time to go home before I had to be down there. As I left Fort Campbell, Kentucky on a plane bound for Chicago, there were many thoughts going through my head. I had some real doubts about my future in the Army and where it would lead me next. I was happy about one thing though. I had managed to escape Vietnam. Several people assured me that the possibility of ending up in Vietnam with my MOS was next to nil. They didn't use HAWK missiles in the jungle. That was reassuring in itself. I did ask where exactly the Army had these missiles, and I was told that most of the units were either in Germany or South Korea. It was a good possibility that I would end up in one of those two places after I finished my training.

I personally was hoping for Germany. At this time in my life I had never traveled outside of the boundaries of the United States other than my short visit to the Bahamas right before entering the Army. The thought of seeing Europe and all of its scenery—including the beautiful women—sounded absolutely fabulous. I spent many hours dreaming about meeting some beautiful blonde German girl and bringing her home to meet my parents. Now that would be my kind of existence in the Army!

Only time would tell whether this dream would come true or not. This sounded much better than crouching in some rice paddy with bullets spraying all around me. I felt reasonably safe as to my future for the first time since I had been drafted against my will. Like I've said before, I was as patriotic as the next guy, but why not be patriotic in the Swiss Alps versus being a dead hero in some rice paddy in a steamy jungle in the middle of nowhere? I wasn't sure about my abilities in air defense, and I wasn't real positive about how things would turn out for the rest of my stay. But at least I had conquered my first fear: staying alive.

Gate Four, Fort Campbell, Kentucky

Post Headquarters, Fort Campbell, Ky.

CHAPTER SEVEN:

The Desert Rat

My first impressions of El Paso, Texas were everything I thought they would be. While flying in from Chicago over the last 200 miles or so, all I could see out of the airplane window was sand, tumbleweed, and more sand. It seemed that there were virtually no towns or cities for miles and miles. I could see right away that El Paso was the perfect place to put a top-secret training center for missiles and air defense. What enemy in his right mind would come clear out here to find anything? It was without a doubt the most desolate and barren country that I had ever seen. I couldn't believe that the Army would even have anything clear out here. It had to be the largest area of absolute nothingness in the entire United States!

As I stepped off the plane in El Paso, the first thing that struck me was how hot and dry it was there. The temperature had to be in the 90's, and it was only early June at 9:00 in the morning. I was immediately looking for some shade and a pair of sunglasses. I could see that the value of these two items would come at a high price in this part of the country. Whether I was going to agree with my Basic Training CO and like this place was still in question. But I was here, and I was going to have to like it or else.

The Army, in all of its efficiency, had a bus at the airport waiting to take prospective missile experts out to Fort Bliss. I thought to myself that if I was any further out in the desert I would be buddies with a cactus or a rattlesnake. After a short ride further out into nothingness, the bus went through the front gate of Fort Bliss. The sign read: United States Army Air Defense School and Training Center. As far as I could see there was nothing out here to defend. Another chapter in my Army life was about to begin.

The following morning brought yet another ridiculously hot day to the sands of western Texas. At 8:00 a.m. sharp, about 100 of us were standing in formation in front of our new home-away-from-home. The Post Commander gave us a short pep talk on the great learning experience that we were about to embark on. He outlined briefly what our training was going to entail, and he stressed that we had all been selected for this training because of our test scores and our obvious abilities. By the time he finished his speech we were all feeling like geniuses. Maybe this was not going to be as bad as I had thought. After all, nothing could be as bad as what I had just gone through over the last three months. Maybe after Basic Training the Army took another approach with its people. Maybe they were going to accept the fact that we were human.

My reverie ended almost as quickly as it began. The Post Executive Officer stepped up in front of us and started his speech by saying the following: "You men are in the worst shape that I have ever seen! Therefore, over the next eight weeks we will see that you are whipped into prime condition that will last you throughout your military careers. To accomplish this, we are going to start a program of speed marches especially designed to get you in shape and bring you up to the expected Army level of combat preparedness!" He went on to say that these marches would be timed, and that the various training Companies would be in competition with each other for the honor of being the top training Company at Fort Bliss.

I couldn't believe what I was hearing! Less than two weeks earlier some jerk from Basic Training had gotten up at our graduation ceremony and told us that we were all in the best shape of our entire lives. Now I had some other jerk standing up there telling me that I was in lousy shape. This had to be the craziest form of psychology that I had ever witnessed. How could you be in great shape in May and be in lousy shape by June?

My earliest thought on all of this was that the only difference between Basic Combat Training and Advanced Individual Training that I could see was a change of location. We still had D.I.'s, and now it looked like they were going to try their darndest to run us into the ground, or sand if you will. I wasn't sure if I was in the Army or the French Foreign Legion. This reminded me of watching Gary Cooper in the movie "Beau Geste." As you might recall in the movie, Gary Cooper was sent to a French Foreign Legion outpost in the middle of the desert of Arabia, and he had to endure the hardships of being in the desert and as far away from civilization as you can get. This is not to mention that he was fighting all of these blood-thirsty nomads and trying to survive his tour with the French Foreign Legion. The only difference was that I couldn't recall being exiled from my country. All I could recall was being drafted!

Amazingly, over time I did manage to find a few differences between BCT and AIT. For one thing, we had air-conditioned barracks. Believe me, when the temperature gets above 100 degrees air-conditioning is a must. How people spend their whole lives out in the desert is beyond me. Spending eight weeks in this kind of environment definitely makes one appreciate the more simple pleasures in life. You just wouldn't believe what the sight of a shade tree does to your mental health when you're standing out in the sand under clear skies in June in El Paso, Texas.

Another difference I noticed was that while the training was still very rigid and structured, there seemed to be a much more relaxed relationship between the D.I.'s and us. There was still a great deal of discipline, but we had a few more laughs along the way. Even the D.I.'s cracked up once in a while. One other major difference was definitely obvious. The guys you were with were definitely brighter than the run-of-the-mill trainee. Most of these guys knew their names and could count to 10 in their heads. Carrying on an intelligent conversation was even a possibility.

My Advanced Individual Training experience brought with it a new place to get used to and a completely new cast of characters. For one thing, in Basic Training everything was done in our fatigues. We were either required to have our fatigue shirts off, such as when we did our hand-to-hand combat and physical training, or we were required to have them on with the sleeves completely rolled down to the wrist. Every big decision, especially those involving our dress code, was made by the D.I. in charge for that day. Trainees never got to think on their own.

At Fort Bliss, we always had our fatigue shirts on but at least we got to have the sleeves rolled up. The only way you would have the sleeves rolled down was in the case of having a bad sunburn. Exposure to the elements was a major concern of the Army's at Fort Bliss, and heat exposure was quite commonplace throughout our training in Texas. It was the belief of our leaders that by simply rolling your sleeves up you could avoid overheating. However, OD Green is a fairly dark color as colors go and as anyone knows, dark colors absorb heat from the sun. White and beige reflect sunlight and heat. Everybody knows this too.

Now you would think that since the brilliant ones in Basic Training had seen it fit to give us all an ample supply of khaki summer clothing that the high-tech geniuses at Fort Bliss would have us wear this same lighter-colored clothing with short-sleeved shirts. Not a chance! Their justification for this policy was that our khaki clothes were not work clothes—they were dress and travel uniforms. The only time that we could wear our khakis was when we were off the Post and were required to wear our uniforms. The only time that this occurred was when we were traveling from one place to another. They wouldn't let you off the Post during work hours except on the weekends, and during the off-hours we weren't required to wear our uniforms. Therefore, we very rarely wore our khakis.

Now if all of this makes sense to you, you're doing better than I am. I didn't understand it then and I don't understand it now. Army policy worked in strange ways. What made things interesting was that the policy changed every place I went. Hazing and harassment, for example, went out the window in AIT. There was very little abuse, either physically or mentally, by the D.I.'s. If you screwed up in the marching or drills the D.I. would simply stare at you with daggers in his eyes. Or they would look at you with one of those disapproving looks that made you think you were in the middle of a nuclear meltdown.

What made this psychology work was that when something happened or somebody messed up, the whole unit would stop whatever they were doing while the D.I. came over to the culprit involved and stared at him for as long as two minutes at a time. Believe me, at 110 degrees in the shade, standing out in the sun without moving can take its toll on even the meanest and most rotten of the litter. Baking to a crisp in the sand with fatigues on is something I would not wish on my worst enemy.

Desire for as much shade as possible did wonders for discipline. The more we screwed up, the less shade time we got. Over an eight-hour day in temperatures above 100 degrees, shade time became a priceless commodity. Therefore, as the training went on we made fewer and fewer mistakes. This pleased the D.I.'s to no end. They probably thought that our getting better at things was a direct result of their brilliant training techniques. If they only knew that it was a sheer will of survival from the sun that made us concentrate better, not their stupid techniques! As I have mentioned before, the group as a whole was much brighter than the one I was with in Basic Training and we went along with just about everything. We would save our laughter and complaints until after working hours.

Going along with everything included going along with the speed marches. These definitely tested our patience and ability to avoid complaining about things. To put it mildly, the concept of speed marches out in the desert to build up our stamina was really difficult to justify in our own minds. We needed speed marches like we needed more OD Green clothing! We went through six of these marches over the eight weeks that we were at Fort Bliss. We started out with 4-milers, and we ended our training with a marathon 12-miler during the last week of training. Whether or not these marches did anything for my stamina or not is truly questionable.

What they did do for me was help me lose the seven pounds that I had miraculously picked up in Basic Training. I had reached the massive weight of 133 pounds by the end of Basic Training. This was as much as I had weighed during my entire life. It took less than two of these marches to sweat out the seven pounds that I had gained. By the end of the eight weeks and the six marches out in the desert, I was back down to my fighting weight of 126. Who knows, maybe the Army planned it that way. It was hard to tell sometimes whether the Army had a plan or not. They certainly wanted you to believe they did.

In any case, I saw some real weird things happen during the course of these six marches. The best way to describe them is to liken them to the Bataan Death March. You know, the famous one that took place in the Philippines during WWII? Don't get me wrong, nobody died on any of these marches. But there were several guys who probably wished they were dead. There was absolutely nothing funny about walking in the desert with a full pack on your back and carrying an M-14 rifle held out in front of you away from your chest. They told us that the M-14 rifle weighed less than 15 pounds. Believe me, after a couple of miles those light rifles felt like they weighed a ton. Some of the healthiest-looking guys in the Company fell apart on these marches. I personally made it through all of them, but it wasn't because I was in better shape than anyone else. What got me through them was probably the same thing that drives people who run in marathons: The accomplishment of finishing the race. It looked bad to fall out of the march. When you fell out of the march, it was as if you had failed to accomplish your mission.

The last thing anybody wanted to be labeled, especially in the Army, was a quitter. Ego played a large role in our lives. The Army had spent weeks working on our egos and making us all believe that we were invincible. Even the hardest to convince eventually came around to this line of thinking. So when it came to the marches, your ego told you that you could make it. Sometimes it worked and sometimes it didn't. I saw a lot of guys with inflated egos fall flat on their faces in the sand. The rest of us with normal egos just kept marching, and most of us made it through to the end of the march.

A prime example of this "inflated ego syndrome" was present throughout the eight weeks that I was in AIT. We had a Platoon of Marines training with us at Fort Bliss. Now don't get me wrong, the U.S. Marine Corps is without a doubt one of the finest organizations within our Armed Forces. However, the Marines, like all branches of our Armed Forces, have their flaws and little quirks that make them unique.

Nowadays in the 21st century, we are constantly barraged with commercials on television and radio extolling the virtues of our various branches of the Service. Whether all of this is just a lot of hype or not is up to each individual. In the 21st century, the Marines say that they want "just a few good men." In the 1970s, it was my belief that they wanted a few good fanatics! This Platoon of Marines that trained with us in the HAWK missile school was not made up of superhumans by any stretch of the imagination. They appeared to be just another collection of regular guys serving their country. However, they had their differences.

The one major difference I observed when comparing the Marines to the Army was the approach that was taken in their training. There seemed to be more zeal and purpose in everything they did. They didn't always succeed in their endeavors, but I must give them credit where credit is due. Without a doubt, these Marines tried harder to break records and finish first more than any of us in the Army. What exactly drove them to these heights is unknown.

I'm sure that if you were to talk to a Marine recruiter on the subject, he would tell you that it is about the "glory of the Service" and its tribute to the Halls of Montezuma and the shores of Tripoli. He would tell you about the many Marines who died heroes in all of our past wars. I had my own theory after observing the Marines for about eight weeks. It was my belief that they were simply scared to death of their Platoon Sergeant! I don't know what these guys go through in their boot camp, but I have never seen a group of guys more scared of screwing up and losing face in my entire life.

I had my share of run-ins with D.I.'s in Basic Training. I also received many attitude adjustment sessions. But through all of this I never got to the point where I was scared of a D.I., and I certainly wasn't scared of making mistakes or failing to accomplish anything. These guys were! You could see it in their eyes. There was a definite fear factor built into their systems. They also suffered from one critical flaw. They all had a horrible case of inflated ego. They all thought they were superhuman.

The best illustration of this inflated ego syndrome came into view during the six speed marches. As you might expect, there were published Post records established for best times out and back for every one of the marches. It was the supreme goal of our Marines to break every one of these established records. They were bound and determined to go down in the history of Fort Bliss, Texas as the greatest training unit ever to go through the U.S. Army Air Defense School. The rest of us normal folks were simply satisfied to get through the training. I, like many of my compatriots, could see no value in being the "best in the West." In fact, the whole idea of it seemed rather absurd. After all, most of us were draftees. We really didn't care whether we left some glorious legacy of our accomplishments behind in the Army. Most of us just wanted to get out as soon as possible. If there was anything that we were gung-ho about in the Army, it was the endeavor of figuring out how to spend as little time in it as possible.

Nobody, I might add, spent more time on this goal than I did. I spent many long hours trying to figure out shortcuts in the system. Any zeal or overachievement that I might have displayed during my Army experience was all directed toward the goal of simply getting back out again all in one piece. I was no hero, nor was I a superhuman. I was just a normal average American who was required to spend some time serving my country. Freedom of any kind had its sacrifices and obligations.

The marches themselves started out easy enough. As I mentioned before, we started with 4-milers. To walk at a fast clip in 90-degree weather in sand halfway up your boots is easier than it sounds. After all, we had been running several miles a day for months at this point. Outside of a few blisters and a couple cases of overexposure to the sun, the Army faired quite well on the 4-mile marches. The Marines, of course, set new records on both, which did not help their ego problems at all. If anything, it made them worse.

The Marines were actually beginning to think they were superhuman! If there was a single Marine in their Platoon who had the slightest doubt about all of this he kept it hidden. Besides, the Platoon Sergeant yelled at them throughout the duration of each march, and it was enough to put cold shivers down anybody's back. This guy was a true fanatic in every sense of the word. He even looked crazy. His head was completely shaved, and he was a perfect human specimen. He was also one mean and nasty son of a bitch! I swore at the time that if anybody ate nails for breakfast this guy did. In all of the time that I spent in the Service, there was nobody that made a lasting impression on me more than this guy. I thought that if we had a few more of these guys around we could win every war without ever firing a shot. He was crazy as shit but impressive nonetheless. There were many times that I was glad he was on our side.

The marches continued throughout the eight weeks of training, elevating to 6 miles, 8 miles, and culminating in the great 12-mile excursion. The Marines continued to break all of the records on every march. They broke the records simply because they were running instead of marching. As the distances got longer and the temperatures during the day got hotter, the desert was taking its toll on everybody—including the Marines. They were still breaking records, but some of them were biting the dust just like the rest of us.

It's a weird feeling marching by a guy laying face first down in the sand. What really struck me in all of this was that their Platoon Sergeant had the balls to stand over the kid screaming at him to get back up and keep running when it was obvious that the kid was close to being completely out of it. I wasn't even sure that the kid could recognize the asshole who was standing over him. It was this kind of display that convinced me that being in the Marines was not all that it was cracked up to be. This was not normal human behavior. This was some scary shit, and I was glad I was not a part of it.

The Army had a far different approach to marching than the Marines. After all, it was their idea. Yes they expected us to complete the marches, but they weren't seriously trying to kill everybody doing it. We took frequent rests along the way. The Army saw to it that anyone who began to not feel well during any of the marches dropped out. In fact, on the last march the Company Commander who was with us on all of the marches stopped us at the 4-mile mark going out. He told us that he had no desire to go any farther himself, and he wasn't going to require any of us to do it either. We all sat down for about an hour or so to kill some time, and then we went back in. Therefore, our 12-mile march ended up being just another 8-mile march. We all thought this was an extremely sensible thing to do. We never set any records, but we had done what we had to do. Besides, when the CO orders you to sit down and quit marching you do exactly what he says.

Following orders is one of the mainstays of military life. It was one thing that I became extremely proficient at during my stay in the Army. The good Captain was not disregarding Army policy; he was simply exercising his option of modification as a leader of men. His decision to not complete the full 12 miles of the march in temperatures over 100 degrees was judged to be very prudent and wise by the rank and file. I felt that if I ever found myself in a combat situation it would be this kind of individual that I would prefer to have leading me into the fray. Common sense in all people is not always evident. I would much rather follow a guy who displays a lot of common sense than follow somebody who simply goes by the regulations no matter how ridiculous they are.

Army regulations and their impact on the normal soldier in 1971 brings back memories of another event that took place during AIT. As I have alluded to many times already, the Army controlled your life with almost every minute detail. How you dressed, how long your hair was, and whether you shaved in the morning or the evening, were just a few of the things that they controlled. In 1971, the Army was going through a lot of in-house changes along with the other branches of the Armed Services. There was a campaign in progress to attract people into the Army for longer stays than just two years. The reenlistment NCO's were hard at work trying to get any of us to commit to a longer time in the Army. And to make the Army life more attractive to prospective enlistees—both men and women alike—many changes were taking place in regard to standards and regulations.

One of the changes was the Army's policy on growing facial hair. Up until 1971, growing a beard or even a moustache was strictly off-limits. This change in the regulations caused a major trend to take place in El Paso, Texas. A few friends and I decided to test the system by growing moustaches, but we were not satisfied to simply grow them. We wanted to see how far we could go with the growth before someone said something to us. Rules are made to test for longevity, aren't they? The Army regulations on the subject stated that while growing a moustache was perfectly fine, there was a limit on how far it could extend on your face. No moustache could extend beyond the corners of the mouth.

Believe me, my friends and I took it to the limit, and in many cases a step further. This obviously did not make us the most popular guys in the Company from the view of our D.I. Our little prank not only made him foam at the mouth, but it eventually delayed our promotion to Private First Class (the usual rank after coming out of AIT). Everybody was usually promoted in AIT. The exceptional trainees made it to the Specialist rank. I, along with my mustached buddies, remained a straight Private after graduation in late July. Our usually congenial D.I. found absolutely no humor in what we had done, and he made sure that we paid for our indiscretion.

He hurt us where it hurts the most—in the pocketbook, because the higher your rank the better your pay. When you are not making much money to begin with, an extra $30 a month can definitely change your lifestyle. He saw to it that ours didn't change until long after we left Fort Bliss. He never once said a thing to us in our daily inspections, but you could just tell that he knew that he was being messed with on this issue. He would just stop in front of each one of us and stare with one of those looks that could stop a clock. We had a lot of good laughs over this in our off-time. It would have been death to laugh while it was happening though. I had a sore tongue for several weeks from biting it too often to keep from laughing. It cost us all some money for a while, but the sheer enjoyment of it was worth every penny.

Our AIT D.I. was really a pretty decent fellow as D.I.'s go. He could take a joke once in a while, and he made the training a lot more fun than it was surely intended to be. Besides our prank with the moustaches, he put up with a lot from us; he could have made it tougher on us if he had wanted to. He just wasn't that bad of a guy.

I must point out here that all D.I.'s acquired nicknames happily bestowed on them by their fearless followers. We called our D.I. "Sugar Bear." You know, the little bear on the Sugar Crisp cereal box? This guy not only looked like the Sugar Bear, but he had many of his attributes. At least we thought so anyway. Just watching this guy walk around with his Mounty-type hat on was one of the funniest things that you could imagine. He used to strut around with this stupid hat on in front of us, continually yelling at us to shape up and do things right or else. Everything he said was funny and had a comical air to it. It was like he was saying it but he didn't seriously expect any of us to believe it. His psychological approach was to try to make us feel bad for not doing things correctly.

The funny part about it was that none of us really cared to get it right in the first place. He could see this himself, but he wasn't about to change his approach midstream. He just kept trying that much harder to convince us of our errant ways. The harder he tried the funnier things got. By the end of our eight weeks, he had just about given up trying to convince us of anything. To make him feel better, we did manage to straighten up and fly right for the graduation ceremony. But you could tell that he knew he had had very little to do with it.

As you can tell by reading this story so far, playing mind games was one of our favorite pastimes in AIT. We used to hone our talents at this in our off-time. There were many sights and diversions in and around El Paso. One of these was Juarez, Mexico. Juarez is just across the border and the Rio Grande River from El Paso. All you had to do was walk across the bridge over the Rio Grande to get there. It was a relatively short bridge as bridges go, but there were some nights that it seemed to be miles long. Stabilizing on Tequila was good for some things and it was lousy for others. Getting back over the bridge after a long evening in Juarez was definitely not one of those things that Tequila was a good antidote for. It often made the short walk back to the United States a major combat mission.

I often wondered whether we learned more military tactics in our schooling or from getting back out of Juarez! There were some evenings when it took every bit of our cunning and military prowess just to get to the bridge. Needless to say, by the end of the eight weeks we were equally adept in both getting in and out of Juarez and arming and disarming HAWK missiles. In the long run, I truly believe that I gained more value out of our exploits in Juarez than I ever gained out of the training I received in AIT. The brilliant tactics we used and devised during these exploits served me well many times over throughout the rest of my brief Army career. The cast of characters that I ran around with during this time were some of the funniest guys that I ever met in the Army. Some of the guys were married, some were engaged, but most of us were still single, unattached, and absolutely crazy individuals. We were willing to try just about anything as long as we didn't end up in jail.

Short of landing in jail, it was as the saying goes, "Katie Bar the Door," when it came to our exploits in Juarez. Now Juarez, Mexico as a place to visit had very few things in it to write home about back then. It was without a doubt one of the dirtiest and most run-down cities that I have ever found myself in. The streets were cluttered and dusty. I would estimate that the biggest industries in town were the drinking establishments and the houses of ill repute. Exactly how many bars and brothels there were in Juarez I never found out, but I would venture to say that our band of merry men managed to hit just about all of them during our eight weeks of training.

I had one friend in particular who I spent more time running around with on these exploits than the others. He was a young man from Plano,

Texas. He was about the same age as I, and he had a wealth of goofy ideas in his head. We thought an awful lot alike, and in spite of our cultural differences we hit it off real well from the beginning. He could speak German, and I had a fairly good knowledge of French and Spanish. We also discovered that we both knew Pig Latin. The two of us came to the conclusion that we could have a blast down in Juarez laying great lines on the girls in the bars. We also figured out that the two of us could communicate back and forth without the girls having the slightest idea of what we were saying. In Pig Latin, we could say just about anything and get away with it. We spent many hours in the bars and on the streets putting out nothing but pure bullshit and having a great time doing it.

We drank more than we should on several of these trips to Juarez, and we often had to help each other back to the United States. It was all in fun and we never really got into any serious situations. We did certainly hassle a lot of girls, and we ate God-knows-what in some of the sleaziest-looking places imaginable. We also had a lot of fun messing with the vendors along the street who tried to sell us just about anything, including their sisters.

Fortunately, neither one of us took them up on any of their offers. It was a well-known fact at Fort Bliss that you could catch all kinds of exotic diseases in Juarez if you weren't careful. The two of us had made a pact very early in our escapades to protect each other from this sort of thing. Some of the other guys in our Company were not nearly as fortunate. The two of us gained some minor fame for our exploits in Mexico among the other guys in the Company. We spent so much time in Juarez that we gained the nicknames of "The Desert Rat" and "Heir Rommel." I was the "Rat" and he was "Rommel."

There were a couple of other events that occurred during our stay at Fort Bliss, Texas that brought some additional humor to our otherwise rigid on-Post existence. Outside of more than a few visits to Juarez and downtown El Paso during the time we were there, there was very little fun involved with the training. What we were learning had nothing to do with fun. We were learning tactics of war and how to handle the machinery of war. The people who were teaching us these things were dead serious, and they expected us to learn it not only well but also for our own preservation.

When you're dealing with missiles with armed warheads on them, there is a very small margin for error. One mistake could get you blown sky-high. The calculations on range and trajectory were also crucial. We were taught to hit every target we shot at. In a wartime situation, misses could mean you were dead instead of the enemy. Making light of any of this training during the classes was strictly taboo. Finding fun had to come from somewhere else besides our training on HAWK missiles.

Besides our training at Fort Bliss, we were all given extra duties such as KP, more commonly referred to as Kitchen Police, and Post guard duty. We were required to do both at least once during AIT. There wasn't much fun in KP, unless you get a charge out of washing pots and pans or peeling hundreds of potatoes. In fact, there wasn't much fun in guard duty either. As it turned out though, humor found its way into this activity for me one night. I had been assigned to guard a Small Weapons Armory on the Post. There were six of us detailed to this duty, with each of us taking a four-hour shift. We had specific orders on how we would guard the Armory, which included exactly how to walk around the building and how many times to do it in your shift.

We also had passwords to prevent unwanted people from entering the Armory unauthorized. We were even given a clip containing five rounds of live ammunition. However, we were instructed to never use our weapons unless a true breach of our security had occurred. We had to yell first and attempt to identify the person or persons trying to get into the Armory. Firing our M-16's was strictly forbidden, except to protect our own lives. Now the odds of ever having anything go wrong while on guard duty in Fort Bliss were next to nil. After all, since this was a classified high-tech training center for HAWK and NIKE-HERCULES surface-to-air missiles there was a tremendous amount of security on the Post already. It wasn't that simple getting on the Post to begin with. So the chances of running into some unsavory character or enemy agent were very slim.

Nonetheless, guard duty, especially at 4:00 a.m., did have a tendency to make you nervous. The slightest sound of any kind had you looking over your shoulder hoping that you wouldn't find anything lurking in the shadows. Now even though we had live ammunition with us, we were not allowed to have it loaded in our rifles. So for all intents and purposes, all you had for protection was an unloaded plastic rifle. To give myself a false sense of security as I walked my Post, I had my rifle set up so that with the slightest motion the locking device that secures the clip in the rifle and loads each round of ammo into position for firing would slam shut, making a noise. Without the clip in the rifle, it did absolutely nothing except make noise. But it gave the impression that you had loaded your rifle and that you were ready to fire it if necessary. I'm sure that if I had run into someone who didn't belong in the area that he would have thought twice about it before he questioned whether I was prepared for him or not.

At around 4:00 a.m., my shift was coming to an end and I had positioned myself to receive my relief for the next shift. What made all of this interesting was that the Army had seen it fit to set this guard duty up so that you didn't know the guy who was going to relieve you. You were required to exchange passwords with him so that you would know that the one relieving you was your actual relief and not some imposter. It was real true-to-life cloak and dagger stuff.

As it turned out, the guy who came to relieve me was a black guy from Alabama. I never saw him coming until the last second. He came out into the light from between a couple of parked trucks. When I saw his shadow I swung around to challenge him with those famous words, "Who goes there?" As I came around, the locking device on my M-16 slammed shut, which scared the living daylights out of my relief. In the dark all I could see were the whites of his eyes, and they were as large as silver dollars at this point. I had scared him so badly that he temporarily forgot what he was supposed to say. All he could say was, "Don't shoot man! I'm your relief!" Well, after a short delay and a few nervous moments, we managed to get through the passwords well enough to establish that he was indeed my relief for the next watch and that I was done for the night. I'm not sure whether he was more scared than I was, but I was glad to be off duty. I made up my mind that night that guard duty was not my cup of tea. All it did for me was make me a nervous wreck! I found a lot of humor in the event when thinking about it later that day. But it wasn't nearly as funny at the time.

As we came to the conclusion of AIT, word got out that everyone in our unit was destined for overseas duty for the duration of our Army careers. Rumor had it that some of us were going to Korea. Regardless, we were all required to go through a series of immunizations for cholera and several other exotic diseases. We had no choice in this matter. Anyone traveling outside the United States for an extended period of time had to get the shots. The first thought I had was that I had spent many extended periods of time in Juarez and nobody had mentioned getting shots because of those trips! I still do not enjoy visits with medical people, and I didn't think too much of doctors at that time in my life either. I wasn't looking forward to getting stuck with a bunch of needles, whatever the reason!

I found out later that I was not alone in thinking that this was a bad idea. The Army thought otherwise, and we were systematically rounded up one morning and marched over to the Infirmary. Once we arrived there, as it usually happened in the Army, we ended up standing in a long line in order to get our immunizations. The line was long enough that it took over an hour to move up into position for the shots. As I got closer to the front of the line I was able to see how they were administering them. There were three orderlies spread out in such a fashion so that one guy was on one side and the other two guys were on the other side. All you had to do was walk down the sidewalk between them and they would nail you as you went along. They were using high-powered needle guns to give you the shots. The guys in front of me explained that each guy who nailed you was giving you several different immunizations at one time. There were about nine different shots that we had to get, if I recall correctly.

What made things worse while standing in line waiting for the shots was that you got to see each guy as he came through the assembly line. Some guys came through totally unscathed by the whole ordeal, while other guys even had the balls to say that it wasn't that bad. You knew they were in pain! There is no way in hell that you can get nine different shots in the course of five seconds and not be in pain.

The trick to not feeling any worse than you had to with these shots was to not tense up prior to getting hit. This was easier said than done. I saw several guys come by who had apparently tensed up right before receiving one of the hits. They had gashes in their arms varying in size from small cuts to cuts that went from the bicep to the elbow. This thing was beginning to look more like some cannibalistic ritual than a series of immunizations. Needless to say, by the time it was my turn to step through the shot line I was as nervous as a cat standing on a bed of hot coals. The first guy I came to told me to just relax and walk through and I wouldn't feel a thing. I was not convinced in the slightest. I asked him how in the world I was supposed to relax while three corpsman were giving me shots in both arms within about five paces? He just shrugged his shoulders, calmly nailed me in the right arm, and told me to go on to the next guy.

By the time I got through the three stations I couldn't lift either arm above my waist. The only thing that I couldn't decide was which arm hurt worse. Everybody was in the same condition as I was after receiving the shots. The Army, bless their souls, had the answer for this problem. To relax everybody's muscles from the shock of the shots, they had us form up. We proceeded to do about 15 minutes of exercises including push-ups and jumping jacks. The brilliance of this idea was overwhelming. By the time we had finished this activity there wasn't a single guy in the Company who could say that he wasn't in pain. As a result of the shots that I had received that day, I had extreme difficulty putting on shirts over the next week. Everybody else had the same problem.

After receiving our immunizations, we were finally ready to begin our Active Duty in the U.S. Army. We had all survived Basic Training, AIT, and even the shot line. We were all in excellent physical shape, no thanks to the speed marches, and we were all highly trained and skilled in the ways of land combat and HAWK missiles. We were now all a part of the Army War Machine. The only question left to be answered was where we would be for the balance of our obligation.

That question was answered for us within the next few days. As I have mentioned before, I was hoping for Germany. But my dreams of running into a beautiful blonde with big boobs and nice legs went out the window in short order. When I picked up my orders from the Company First Sergeant they read "ASCOM, Inchon, Korea, Transient Company, 8th United States Army." What made things worse was that I was going to have to be there within three weeks. It suddenly dawned on me that I would be celebrating my 23rd birthday in a foreign country. The thought of this thrilled me to no end.

Now over the past few years, I had not gotten too excited about my birthday. As you get older, the significance of the event becomes less important in the grand scheme of things. But the thought of spending your birthday in some other country was another thing altogether. I wasn't sure that I was prepared for that or not. It was something that I still had to work out in my mind.

Trauma was setting in fast, and I couldn't stop it. I was falling into a depression at a fairly rapid rate. I could find absolutely nothing to be happy about. I had 19 months left in the Army, and now I was going to some place that I knew practically nothing about. Oh, I had read about Korea in textbooks and I had an uncle who had been in Korea in the 1950s during the Korean Conflict, but my knowledge of this place was very limited at best. The only thing I knew for sure about Korea was that it was near Japan and that it had a lot of mountains. I also knew that the United States had had an occupation force over there for many years.

I was also informed during my HAWK missile training that Korea was strategically a crucial part of our country's defense plan. I wasn't going to one of the hottest spots in the world as far as risking my life went, but I had gotten the impression that it was a damned important military installation. If it ever did get hot over there, it would happen in a hurry! North Korea had a standing army of many thousands of men poised to come over the border into South Korea on a moment's notice. The threat of a Communist takeover and an attack from North Korea were ever-present realities. Some 20 years had gone by since there had been any serious fighting over there, but an uneasy peace still existed in Korea in August 1971. In less than three weeks I was going to become a part of that very real and uneasy peace. At the time I thought to myself, "Brother—you're in the Army now!"

CHAPTER EIGHT:

Korea or Bust

The many stepping stones along the way throughout my brief Army career were beginning to have all the makings of an excellent travelogue. In five short months I had gone from Chicago to Kentucky, to Texas, and now I was headed for the great state of Washington near Seattle. The next stop was Fort Lewis, Washington, which was situated and in view of Mount Rainier in all of its majestic glory.

Through the method of pre-arrangement, Heir Rommel and I had agreed to meet in Seattle ahead of time and do some partying before we were expected to be at the Transient Center at Fort Lewis. We had both thought that a little entertainment for one night was definitely in order since we were headed for the same fate. We were leaving the good old United States for an undetermined amount of time. We met at the airport, found a motel for one night, and started inquiring as to where two lonely American boys could find a good time before we were required to go back to the doldrums of Army life.

Before we left the airport we walked by the Hertz rent-a-car desk. The girl behind the counter was an absolutely gorgeous brunette with a beautiful set of legs. Heir Rommel and I immediately decided that this girl was the obvious one to ask about where all the good spots in town were for having a good time. The way she looked and carried herself gave us the idea that if anyone knew where the nightspots were she would. Through our many escapades in El Paso and Juarez, we had developed quite a flair for striking up conversations with members of the opposite sex. So without further adieu, we came right out and asked her where the best spot in town was for entertainment.

The woman's first response floored us both immediately and left us speechless for at least 30 seconds. She said with an absolutely engaging smile, "Why don't you guys go to my place?" Neither one of us expected this response. We both heard that the girls of the great Northwest were friendly, but this was ridiculous! We knew we had developed some good lines for women but they weren't *that* good. We hadn't even laid any of the good stuff on her and she was already inviting us to her place for the evening.

The only thing we could come up with was, "Have you got another friend for a foursome?" She gave us a funny look for a minute before she realized what we were thinking. After a few more seconds of undisturbed anxiety on both her part and ours, she managed to straighten out our line of thinking. She said she hadn't meant "her place," but instead a bar named My Place, which was just down the street from the motel where we had decided to stay. She was obviously terribly embarrassed by all of this, and to say the least, so were we. After fumbling a few more stupid lines of apology to her we decided that it was a good time for a calculated retreat.

I'm not sure who was more relieved—her or us—but in any case we left the airport in short order and at a double-time march! We did manage to get the directions to My Place and the motel in spite of the uncomfortable position that we had put ourselves in. After checking in at the motel, we headed for the bar to discuss our stupidity over a couple of beers. Actually, we were really a couple of nice guys. Yes, we were out to have some fun and maybe do a little dancing with girls. And sure we were up for whatever else might develop as the night went along, but we weren't exactly soliciting for uninhibited sex! We were just a couple of clean-cut all-American boys! What harm was there in having a little fun before we went off to war?

I still wonder sometimes how far things would have gone if we had gone a step further with the Hertz girl. I mean after all, she sure gave us the impression that she was embarrassed by our inquiries. But that beautiful set of legs and the way the rest of her looked certainly would give anyone the impression that she was definitely not naïve when it came to socializing with men. She was one fine-looking girl! Without a doubt she probably had many fine-looking friends as well.

That was our first defeat in the war with the opposite sex, and we had lost our strategic position without firing a shot! It took us the rest of the evening to recover from our hasty retreat from the front lines. After a couple of beers, Heir Rommel and I decided that the encounter really hadn't counted. We still possessed our many talents in covert operations and that had obviously been a fluke. We had simply been temporarily out-maneuvered. The general attack plans were still brilliant, and there was no doubt that we would win the battle of the day in the end. Undaunted and given newfound confidence by the beers we drank, we pressed onward and upward in our pursuit of a good time for the night.

During our lengthy stay at My Place we managed to consume several beers, many of which were bought by a couple of Vietnam vets we began talking with earlier in the evening. They must have felt a sense of patriotism once they found out we were in the Army and that we were about to embark on overseas duty. In fact, the only beers we paid for all night long were the two we originally had to recover from our strategic retreat from the Hertz girl.

It turned out to be a great evening, and we did our share of drinking and dancing with girls. The following morning gave testimony to our great successes of the night before. We both had the worst hangovers that either one of us could recall. We were both in superb shape when we arrived to process-in at Fort Lewis. We had survived our last civilian fling in the United States before embarking on the wilds of Korea. Our heads hurt so badly that there was nothing the Army could do to us that could make us feel any worse than we already did. We were fully prepared for whatever the Army could deal out.

The processing-in at Fort Lewis went the same way that it did in every other place I had been to so far in the Army. It turned out to be an all-day project. There were hundreds of guys heading for overseas duty, and waiting for your name to be called to review your orders and records was nothing unusual. Having names that were alphabetically toward the end of the list, Heir Rommel and I ended up having nearly the whole morning to recover from our hangovers. We met up with many of the guys from our unit at Fort Bliss, and we spent the morning catching up with all of the news and rumors on where everybody was going to end up spending the rest of their time in the Army. By the time that my name was called I had fully recovered from the previous night's activities. I still wasn't thrilled with the idea of leaving the country, but I was at least ready to find out where I was going to have to spend the next year or so of my life.

Much to my disappointment, I was still headed for Korea. Nothing had happened in the past two weeks to change my destiny. The Army was bound and determined to see that I was headed for points unknown and would definitely remain a HAWK Missile Launcher Crewman. God only knew what made me think that the Army would come to their senses and do something else with all of my obvious talents. The Army had made a drastic mistake, and at this point I saw nothing in the cards that was going to change my situation. I was stuck and I knew it.

Going AWOL was a thought, but with all of the military police around it was strictly out of the question. Besides, I didn't have enough money to get very far anyway. I was just going to have to make the most of the situation. I was intelligent. This was no time to turn into an idiot. Surely my brainpower would get me through this mess one way or another. It was only a matter of time before the Army would realize its error and put me somewhere where my journalistic talents would be utilized, right?

I had great faith in my assessment of the situation, and in spite of the overwhelming evidence that the Army thought that I should be a Missile Launcher Crewman I still felt like something would happen along the way that would change the whole program. I based all of this on the many stories I heard about the Army doing things in strange ways. Everything was subject to change at any time. Nothing was permanent in the Army except the fact that you had to serve your time once you were drafted.

My belief in this theory carried me through the many hours of depression that I felt throughout my stay at Fort Lewis. Waiting around to leave the country for who- knows-where was not an uplifting mental experience. Joking around with your friends and trading war stories did not fill all of the many hours that we spent waiting for our turn to leave the country. Playing cards and going to movies on the Post were the highlights of what turned out to be almost a week in Fort Lewis. We were a captive audience, and there wasn't much else to do while we waited. By the end of the week I had become a proficient Spades player. Some of our games lasted well into the early hours of the morning, leaving only enough time to sleep a few hours before we started the next game.

The Army, in all of its wisdom, did manage to find a few things for us to do during our stay at Fort Lewis. The geniuses realized that boredom was a very large issue while we waited for our shipping papers. They made us show up daily for two formations, one in the morning and one in the late afternoon. I think the only purpose of these formations was to see if anyone had run off or not. All they did was take roll call and let us go on our merry way. The night of my fourth day at Fort Lewis was highlighted by my having to pull guard duty. No one had a choice when it came to participating in this activity. It was standard procedure at Fort Lewis to use the temporary manpower that flowed through the Fort for those duties that the regularly assigned soldiers didn't want to have anything to do with.

Now from what I had seen of Fort Lewis during my first three days there, I couldn't think of anything that needed guarding. After all, this was simply a Transient Center full of buildings that contained nothing but administrative equipment and personnel. The largest amount of anything that I had observed so far was typewriters. Most of these were government-issued manual typewriters that nobody would be overly interested in. There was the Mess Hall, but the food that was served there was also government-issued and certainly not gourmet. They did have a Detention Center on the Post, but with the sizeable number of military police around, I couldn't imagine them needing any help from a bunch of guys just out of training. As it turned out, they didn't need our help. They just needed some suckers to do their most undesirable job for them.

I learned something new while on guard duty that night at Fort Lewis. There were four different kinds of discharges that you could get from the Army: honorable, dishonorable, undesirable, and general. Honorable discharges were easy to get. Most everybody who went into the Army at the time and returned to civilian life without any major military mistakes got one. The last three categories were very rare. To end up with a dishonorable discharge from the Army meant that you had done something absolutely horrible such as killing a fellow soldier or committing treason or something. The last two kinds of discharges were similar to the dishonorable type except that they were less severe in their repercussions. They were saved for those types of individuals who just didn't fit into the Army's scheme of things.

Judging by some of the guys who I had already observed in the Army, this organization fit practically everyone into the system one way or another. Being a little strange or having a few little quirks of one kind or the other was the norm for the Army. In fact, I was almost totally convinced that I was one of the very few perfectly normal human beings in the organization. So I just couldn't imagine anyone ending up with either of the last two kinds of discharges. To my amazement, however, I found out that there were several of these kinds of guys being housed at the Detention Center at Fort Lewis. All of those people getting out of the Army less- than-honorably were called "212's." I found out that to be called a 212 was worse than being called a trainee. This group of folks was definitely the scum of the earth in the eyes of the Army—212's were barely considered human at all.

It was this group of "sub-humans" that I was assigned to watch over that night. For the most part, the night of guarding the "bad boys" went without event. We were given two-hour shifts throughout the night, which consisted of simply standing outside the outer door of the Detention Center and keeping your eyes open. We never got close to the bad boys themselves so the whole affair was rather boring. Outside of hearing a few cat-calls from inside the cellblock, nothing of great interest occurred during my couple of shifts. The whole experience did nothing for my outlook on things except that I decided that going out of the Army honorably was the only way to go. If nothing else, the night of guard duty broke up the monotony of card-playing and trading war stories for a while. In fact, if one had a vivid imagination several new war stories could be created from having to guard the 212's. I tried not to get involved in this sort of thing myself.

I spent the major portion of the following day sleeping off the effects of guard duty. I did get into some more card-playing before the day was over, but even that was starting to become a real bore. Besides, in spite of my expertise in Spades and Hearts I lost my shirt. Fortunately, we never played for money in these card games. The only thing that I really lost was part of my ego. We were all getting a little testy and the anxiety level was rising steadily as each day went by without any word as to when we were due to depart for the Orient.

Finally on the sixth day of internment at Fort Lewis, our group of guys finally got the word that we were shipping out the next day. We had to pack all of our things and move to another area, which was six blocks down the road from where we had been for the past few days. This move to another barracks made very little sense because we all knew that where we had been all week was right on top of the staging area for the outgoing buses to the airport. We had all been watching the guys leave for the airport all week long. In fact, we all had remarked on how lucky we had been to be assigned a barracks so close to where the buses were loaded. Carrying one's belongings over great distances had become a consistent chore for all of us over the past several months, and any chance to shorten the distance was looked upon as having truly rare luck. So much for luck! Most of us took the stand that having to move everything again was nothing but pure bullshit and another way for the Army to fill up half of our last day at Fort Lewis.

The following morning we marched back those six blocks with all of our stuff and boarded buses to go to the airport. We were taken to McCord Air Force Base near Tacoma, Washington, given a box lunch, and loaded onto a Braniff International Airways jet for our flight to Korea. At about noon on Aug. 9, 1971, we took off and left the United States for the next 13 months. The flight took us first to Anchorage, Alaska, where we stopped for refueling and to stretch our legs and so forth. During my 40-minute stay in Alaska I observed pretty much what I had expected Alaska to be like. It was about 35 degrees outside with a steady drizzle coming down. It was also extremely windy that day, which did nothing for my opinion about living in a place like that. As we flew in, I also noticed that there was still a lot of snow on the peaks of the mountains around Anchorage. I thought to myself, "Do they ever have summer up here?" From the looks of it, the answer to this question was a definite no!

I wasn't disappointed when they ordered us back onto the plane to take off again. I wasn't anxious to leave the country or anything, but this last view of the United States territory had put a real damper on the day's events. I was already about half-sick over this whole thing and they didn't serve any booze on military flights. Flying was not new to me, but I never have been overly comfortable with it. I just have this thing about someone else controlling my life for even short periods of time. Having a few drinks along the way never hurts the butterfly population. For me, flying without a few stabilizers in your belly is nerve-wracking to say the least.

The next portion of our trip to Korea did nothing to make me feel any more at ease. The next stretch in the air lasted approximately eight hours. We flew from Anchorage, Alaska to Tokyo, Japan. Our pilot, once we were in the air and leveled out again, calmly came over the intercom and notified us that we were now at 38,000 feet and that we would stay at that attitude throughout the flight. In an attempt to be funny, he also suggested that none of us should step outside without our coats on since it was about minus 50 degrees outside of the plane. I was so nervous that the thought of getting out of my seat was bad enough, let alone stepping outside of the plane. I must say though, the flight over the Pacific Ocean was really quite smooth and uneventful. I even managed to calm down a little and dozed off and on between card games.

I was relatively back to normal after a few hours in the air, and I even ventured out of my seat once or twice during the flight. I felt fine until the pilot announced that we were approaching Tokyo, Japan and that we would be landing soon. We were all ordered back to our seats and told to strap ourselves in for landing. The way this was handled by our leaders sounded quite ominous. Now our pilot had done a positively beautiful job of flying the plane over the ocean. However, my faith in him left me almost immediately after his announcement of our impending landing.

Less than five minutes after we had all sat down and put our seat belts on, the plane took a sharp left turn at a 45-degree angle and started into a downward altitude. The hard bank to the left and down put my stomach into my throat, and I was sure we were heading for a crash-landing several miles short of the runway. My first thought was that the pilot had kicked the bucket and the co-pilot didn't know how to land the plane. You know how they say that when you think you're going to die your whole life flashes in front of your eyes? Well, all nine of mine went by several times during this landing in Japan.

Somehow or another we managed to hit land and made it down on the runway at Yokota Air Base near Tokyo, Japan. During the flight we had crossed the International Dateline somewhere over the Pacific. We landed in Japan at around 3:15 p.m. on the 10th of August, 1971. It was extremely hot and muggy when we got off the plane for the refueling process. The perspiration began to flow as soon as we got out into the air outside of the plane. Heir Rommel came to the rescue for all of us by making his usual quips about the scenery and the local people. He had a knack for being funny in the things he said even under the worst conditions. Here we were, all standing around in this awful heat sweating bullets and trying to recover from jet lag, and this guy was cracking jokes right and left. He did the same thing on our speed marches at Fort Bliss. Comic relief after our harrowing landing in Japan was very much needed by all of us though. By the time we had to board the plane again for the rest of our trip, we were all back in a fairly jovial mood.

The next stop in our trek was Korea. After another three hours in the air our fearless pilot made another historic landing, this time at Kimpo Air Base near Seoul, Korea. This time we came in straight but in complete cloud cover. It was the monsoon season in Korea and it was raining cats and dogs. I was doing fine on this landing until this clown came out of the clouds. When we ducked under the cloud cover we were already at treetop level. I was sure that he was going too fast to land and stop this thing before the end of the runway. Miraculously, he did everything right and we were finally on the ground in Korea. I was never so relieved in my life to get off an airplane. I was actually happy to be in Korea, which was one of the craziest thoughts I had ever had.

It was about 7:00 p.m. now. Before leaving the Air Base, we did some preliminary processing-in and had to change the rest of our American money into Korean and military "funny money." Funny money looked like the money found in the Monopoly board game. Technically, we were not supposed to use any American money in Korea. All currency had to be converted to either Korean Wan or this military funny money. However, once in a while the locals in the country would take our American currency. How they disposed of it we never asked. We later boarded buses again and were driven through the Korean countryside to the 199th Replacement Station near Inchon, Korea. After an additional tedious two hours of processing-in and lugging our now rain-soaked gear around, we finally were escorted to our new home-away-from-home. After nearly 24 hours of flying and bus-riding here and there and standing in lines for various reasons, we were finally allowed to get some sleep.

My Korean adventure was about to unfold. I was looking forward to it, and then again maybe I wasn't. In any case, I had the next 13 months to make my mind up on the subject. It was definitely going to be an experience. What kind of an experience I wasn't sure, but at this point I was too worn out to think about it. A good night's rest would surely bring a better day and more insight.

CHAPTER NINE:

I'm Going to Be a What?

I have already alluded earlier to the lifestyle endured at the U.S. Army Transient Centers. The 199th Replacement Company at ASCOM near Seoul, Korea offered no new surprises. There were hours and hours of idle time to contend with both day and night. The Army simply had nothing for us to do. All we could do was sit around and wait for our turn to be assigned to a permanent duty station. What made this particular place more miserable than the others I had already been in was the weather.

From about July to October every year, Korea experiences a rainy season commonly referred to as the "monsoon season." It's like taking a continuous shower for four to five days after somebody used up all of the hot water before you got in there. During this entire season you are never dry. Your skin feels clammy and your clothes are constantly sticking to you. The air is thick enough to cut with a knife. Breathing becomes labored, and your energy level reaches an all-time low. Even your mental processes slow to a crawl and life becomes a listless existence. It's probably very close to the feeling that people get when they are put into the situation of being shipwrecked on the open sea in a life raft. You drift for hours and even days with no change in scenery. After so long, you begin to wonder if this will ever have an ending to it. No matter how upbeat you are, after a few days you are mentally demoralized. All of your hopes of a bright and new future gradually go by the wayside, and you sink into despair.

I was in the 199th Replacement Company for only four days, but it seemed like an eternity. With the rain coming down 24 hours a day, taking long walks to uplift my spirits was definitely out. I was trapped inside a Quonset hut. Everything got old in a hurry! I was sick of playing cards, but I found myself playing anyway just to fill the time. I never passed up opportunities to make a little money. Casual reading wasn't the answer either. I usually lost interest and concentration in what I was reading after just a few pages. I did manage to send off a few letters while I was there, but I can just imagine what the people I sent them to thought when they read my vivid descriptions of where I was and how I was feeling at the time. The monotony of the whole situation really had me down.

I drowned my sorrows every evening for a few hours at the local NCO Club. Beer and mixed drinks were cheap, and for about $3 or $4 you could damn near forget where you even were! These nightly excursions were the sheer highlight of the 199th Replacement Company. I will touch on this as we go along further in the story, but I must tell you that the NCO Clubs in foreign countries at the time had one of the greatest secrets that our military establishment has ever conceived of to keep the morale of the men up in troubled times—GIRLS!

Those evenings at the NCO Club at ASCOM allowed me to have my first experience of socializing with women of Asian descent. Up to this point in my life, I could honestly say that I had never been really slick at attracting women. I think my height and slender build were always factors in this endeavor. Finding short attractive women was always a problem. Plus, I wasn't real good at coming up with dazzling one-liners either. However, in Korea being short was "in." I soon found out that I fit in with the girls just fine. They were all my size! You didn't need a wealth of one-liners to dazzle them with either because they couldn't understand half of what you said anyway. It was also very easy to remember their names. Practically every girl I ran into was either named Jeanie or Miss Lee. Mr. Lee must have been a very busy little devil! Also during these first couple of days in Korea, I came to the conclusion that Asian women have the finest leg structure of any woman in the world. And being a "leg-man," I was in seventh heaven!

Most of the girls in these NCO Clubs were local "talent" from the surrounding villages around the Army Posts. The Army, in all of its wisdom, allowed the local girls to frequent the on-Post clubs to mingle with the troops. Now don't get the wrong idea. These were not Army-organized houses of ill repute. However, they didn't prevent you and some gal from going off-Post to her place for the evening either. More on this later...

During my third day of internment in the 199th Replacement Company, I was called to the Personnel office. It was during this visit that I received another one of many shocks as to the military's way of thinking. When I reported to the Personnel Sergeant he had my file lying open in front of him. We went through the standard questions as to my age, education level, military and civilian skills, and so forth. He noted that I had a very high clerical score from those idiot tests that I had taken when I first entered the Army. He also verified that I could type. After about 20 minutes of going through all of these boring facts, the old sarge really floored me with his next proclamation. He stated that even though I was a highly skilled and trained Missile Launcher Crewman for HAWK surface-to-air missiles they were going to make me a clerk. I couldn't believe it!

After eight weeks of standing in the hot sun of El Paso, Texas making an effort to really learn all of the technical inner workings of HAWK missiles, these jerks were now going to use me as a clerk simply because I had a college degree, I could type, and I had a high clerical score on some test that I really questioned the validity of in the first place. This was truly a fine example of tax dollars at work. Eight weeks of wasted training at God knows what cost, all over a few overlooked lines in my file. It was quite obvious (to me, anyway) from looking at my background before entering the Service that I should have been trained as a clerk from the beginning. Now don't get me wrong. I wasn't unhappy about learning of these great military plans for me. I had not been looking forward to walking guard duty on some TACH site in the middle of Nowhere, Korea for the next 13 months. If anything, I was elated beyond belief at this new turn of events. But I just couldn't understand how it had happened.

This decision by the Army would go on to change my whole perspective about coming to Korea and being in the Army in general over the next 13 months. This whole affair was beginning to take a turn for the better from my point of view. After all, how many clerks get killed in action? Whoever heard of a typewriter blowing up accidentally or being a prime military target for destruction? I was actually beginning to have a false sense of security that the Army was really looking out for my best interests.

Even the continuing rain outside from the monsoons didn't put a damper on my rising spirits. I walked back to the barracks and got thoroughly soaked, but I enjoyed every minute of it. I celebrated my good luck at landing a clerk's job that night at the NCO Club. I danced with every Miss Lee I could find, not even noticing whether she was ugly or not. This whole feeling of euphoria carried over to the next morning because I didn't even notice that I had my usual headache and upset stomach from too much booze and beer. I was able to pack up my gear and prepare to move to bigger and better things in the Army without even a hitch or the slightest thought of failure in the upcoming future. I was ready to attack the enemy with a renewed vigor and self-confidence that I hadn't felt for quite some time.

CHAPTER TEN:

Army Life Isn't So Bad After All

On Friday, August 13, 1971, I was off to my newly assigned permanent duty station: Headquarters Battery, Second Battalion, 71st Air Defense Artillery Unit, 38th Brigade, 8th United States Army. I was heading for Camp Red Cloud, which was in a small village called Uijongbu, Korea. According to the Personnel people at ASCOM, this village is about 20 miles north of Seoul, the capital of South Korea. My unit was being housed at Camp Red Cloud, which was an I-Corp installation (An I-Corp was a unit made up of jobs in the military such as infantry units and the like). Our HAWK Battalion was a separate and independent unit outside of I-Corp that shared the facilities at Camp Red Cloud. We often coordinated our activities with this other unit, and we were expected to follow whatever guidelines they had established for the Post. Our unit had no connection with I-Corp outside of being on its Post, which would have an interesting impact on things as I would find out later in my stay in Korea. I was also informed that from a military standpoint I would be approximately 10 air seconds from North Korea.

I didn't realize the significance of this fact until much later in my hitch. But believe me, when it did dawn on me how close I was to North Korea and the enemy it had a dramatic effect on my life and the way I view things even to this day. The story behind this revelation will be discussed later, but I can tell you that it was a very humbling experience. It is one I will never forget for as long as I live.

I arrived at HQ Battery, Camp Red Cloud at around 10:00 a.m. and began my processing-in. I was escorted from department to department by a SP/5 (Specialist Fifth Class) out of Personnel. The processing-in went pretty much the same as it had in the many places I had been to already—except for one small fact. It seemed to be going a hell of a lot faster than I had previously experienced. All of the clerks here were not only friendly, but they actually seemed to be intelligent and highly efficient. I was swept through the processing-in phase in about 90 minutes flat, and I found myself standing in front of the Battery First Sergeant at 11:30 in the morning. My escort from the Personnel department was telling the First Sergeant that I was the clerk they had been expecting for the past two weeks. Judging by the way this whole conversation was going, I began to get the impression that something was amiss but I couldn't put my finger on it. I dismissed my building anxiety as the First Sergeant told me he was glad to have me in the unit. He told me to relax, go to lunch at the Mess Hall up the street, and report back to him at 1300 hours for further processing-in. There was something funny going on here, but damned if I could figure out what it was.

After a remarkably good lunch at the Mess Hall, I reported back to the First Sergeant in the Orderly Room. In an attempt to keep things going well I showed up 10 minutes early. At precisely 1300 hours, I was again sent off with my SP/5 escort from Personnel to finish my processing-in. After going to a couple of additional departments including the Armorer to issue me my M-16 and ID, I was done with my processing-in. It being Friday and all, my escort told me as we walked back to the Orderly Room that I was done for the day and probably the weekend. The First Sergeant confirmed this upon our return to the Orderly Room. He told me to report the following Monday morning at 0800 to begin work.

My first day at my permanent duty station was ending at 2:30 in the afternoon. As I walked up to the barracks with the Personnel guy, I was still wondering about this quickie processing-in I had just experienced. He could tell by my expression that I was totally perplexed by this whole affair. He had the look of a cat that had just swallowed a canary. I finally couldn't resist it anymore and asked if I had missed something along the way.

As it turned out, according to my new buddy in Personnel, they had known about my presence on this earth for the past two weeks or so. It seemed that the Army put out a manifest of all incoming personnel and then sent these lists out to the various units to let them know how many and what kind of trained men they could expect to receive month to month to replace the outgoing guys. These manifests contained a lot of information on these men, including their skills, age, education level, and so forth. The guys in Personnel for the Battery worked closely with the guys in the Brigade office in Osan, Korea. With a little under-the-table maneuvering and trading off one guy for another, the various Battery Personnel people could practically handpick who they received for replacements. This is how I ended up coming to Camp Red Cloud. I got into some of this trading and maneuvering myself later on in my stay at HQ Battery, which I will describe in a later chapter.

By the end of the evening of my first day, I had received the whole story as to how I ended up in the unit I was now in. According to further reports, it seemed that at the time of my entry onto the manifest for incoming personnel at HQ Battery, 2nd, 71st, ADA, it was in need of two types of people over the next few months of 1971. They were in need of 16D10's and clerical types. As I found out as time went on, 16D10's were fairly easy to find, but finding clerks with good typing skills was another story. What complicated this for the Battery was that the NCO's and the clerks in Personnel had a fondness for college graduates to fill their need for clerks. It didn't take me too long to discover that at least in this unit, the clerks and the NCO's pretty much ran everything from an administrative standpoint. In other words, if the clerks decided to goof-off nothing would get done at all.

As the story went on, it had more of a cloak-and-dagger feel the further it went. Apparently, HQ Battery had a mail clerk who was getting "short," which meant that he was less than 30 days from leaving the country. He was getting desperate to find a replacement for himself. Each clerk had to make an effort to find his own replacement with the help of Personnel. The officers of each section left it pretty much up to their clerks to approve or disapprove of their own replacements.

In any case, his search brought me into the picture for his possible replacement. It was generally concluded by all involved in this search that even if I didn't work out for this guy's replacement, the Personnel department was not going to let me out of HQ Battery. They were going to use me someplace no matter what. One thing was for sure: there were no plans for me to ever work as a Missile Launcher Crewman from almost the very day of my graduation from Air Defense School! At least the guys in Korea had it planned that way. I'm sure that the instructors at the school would be up in arms if they found out what the Army was really doing with its highly trained graduates.

With all of this in mind, I headed into the weekend with a newfound interest in the Army's way of life. I was still a little anxious about everything and how exactly it was all going to turn out in the long run. So far though, everyone was real nice and it seemed that this "permanent party gig" was a complete reversal of what I had experienced in the first few months of my time in the Service. Everything was laid- back and relaxed here in Korea, and the only places you really had to run to were the Mess Hall and the NCO Club. The Post to which I was assigned was really beautiful, and the scenery surrounding Uijongbu was breathtaking. I knew that the first real need I had was for a good camera.

Looking at Camp Red Cloud, you would never know that you were within just a few miles of the DMZ and Communist North Korea. This was crazy—there was even a par-3 golf course right on the Post. I was already thinking that this wasn't going to be so bad after all. The only thing I could see that was missing on this Post was American girls. In fact, there were no women on the Post at all. There were plenty in the village of Uijongbu, however, as I would soon discover.

CHAPTER ELEVEN:

How to Be a Mail Clerk or Some Other Kind of Clerk in Three Easy Lessons

One of the first things that had to be endured when you arrived in a foreign country in the Army's scheme of things back then was the local indoctrination. It is similar to college fraternity hazing with a few minor differences. For one thing, you had to spend countless hours listening to the guys who had been in the country longer than you tell you that they were "short" and that you literally had eons of time left to go. After a few sessions of this, you began to get the mentality that you may very well spend the rest of your life in this God-forsaken existence. As it turned out, the hazing died down after about a month or so. But for a while, it seemed like it was going to go on forever.

Another part of the indoctrination included being introduced to the local people living around the Post. This, of course, was an integral part of your initial training in the job or jobs that the Army, in all of its wisdom, had decided was right for you. You see, in order for you to do your job properly in a foreign country, you had to understand the local customs so that you didn't offend anyone. After all, you were a guest of sorts and a certain amount of decorum had to be maintained at all times. In other words, you wanted to stay out of the local jails!

During my first few weeks in Korea, I was told practically every day by at least one or two people that—whatever you did—stay out of the Korean jails. If you by some chance ended up in one you were literally on your own and the Army could not save you or bail you out of trouble. I heard numerous horror stories—true or not—about what could happen to you if you messed around and got into trouble with the civilian Korean authorities. This was really a serious thing and was not to be taken lightly. Not that G.I.'s in a foreign country, many of whom were away from home for the first time in their lives, would do anything that was against the law or anything.

Good old American pranks, as we considered them, didn't always sit well with our Korean hosts. But after you are in a country for a while you have a tendency to forget that you could really get into trouble with the locals. Besides, the situation in Korea was so different from what you might expect from regular everyday American life. The environment we were in could almost overwhelm you, particularly when it came to what was accepted as normal behavior. In 1971, Korea was a relatively backwards country compared to the United States. Yes, they had modern highways, high-rise buildings, gas stations, and so forth, but they were all built either during the Korean Conflict or shortly thereafter. Korea was more like the United States during the 1940s and 1950s. It was my belief back then that the U.S. Military's presence during the Korean Conflict was the only reason Korea was modern at all.

While there were some larger cities such as Seoul and Osan, for the most part, Korea was a very rural and rundown country. Every so often you would run across a small village or town with open-air markets and a few business establishments, but they were nothing like what we were used to in the States. Garbage collection, indoor toilets, and plumbing were at a premium. Running water was almost nonexistent. Most of the housing consisted of walled-off courtyards with elevated cubicles spaced along a wooden deck. Many families lived together, including Grandma and Grandpa, and in some cases, cousins, uncles, and aunts too. Heating was provided by charcoal bricks shoved under the floors of these cubes, and cooling was provided by the open air except for an occasional fan if electricity was available. Outhouses were quite common. Most of the streets were dirt roads or brick pathways. There were a few sidewalks here and there, but for the most part, once you left the military Posts with all of their modern conveniences it was like stepping back in time to an earlier age.

Every military Post in Korea had a village of locals connected with it that I imagine sprung up upon the arrival of the military. Wherever the Army was, there was money to be made for the locals. Every village had several bars and little shops at which vendors were selling a large variety of things to trap the G.I.'s into spending their money on. You could buy practically anything 50 yards beyond the Post gates. "Black marketing" was a common activity. Many of the locals were dependents of former G.I.'s. Some even had PX privileges like we did. So every time deliveries were made to stock up the PX, there were lines of dependents snatching up cigarettes, beer, toiletry items, cameras—you name it—to sell out in the village on the Black Market. If you were adept at bargaining you could really get some good deals on stuff out in the village.

Camp Red Cloud was situated near the town of Uijongbu, Korea. It was a "bustling" town of about 5,000 people. If you traveled far enough into town there were a variety of things to do. These included a rundown movie house, where you could watch year-old American flicks dubbed in Korean, as well as local productions. If you were into walking, you could really get the flavor of Korean society. You never got too far off the Post most of the time though. If you intended to sightsee, you had to go in groups to avoid all of the Mamasans who were trying to sell their daughters for hire. Oh yes, there were many brothels available if you were so inclined. This barrage of selling usually took place as soon as you walked out the Post gates.

The only thing that really curtailed this was the fact that there was a curfew at midnight when everyone had to be off the streets. This curfew occurred between the hours of midnight and 0600 by Korean law. They didn't care where you were as long as you were off the streets. This was usually how G.I.'s got into trouble with the authorities though. Once in a while, guys drank too much or beat up their girlfriends or didn't properly pay for a girl's services. But for the most part, everyone was out for a good time and stayed out of trouble.

We had our own entertainment provided by the Army on the Post too. We had a Service Club for the troops where you could drink and listen to music or watch TV and relax. There was a library, a movie house, a swimming pool, a golf course, tennis courts, and so forth. It was really quite nice and almost like home. The PX store was always well-stocked with groceries, snacks, pop, beer, toiletries, etc. So for the most part, you could survive quite well for 13 months. We had a great Mess Hall for all of our meals. They even had a snack shop that was open until 2200 or 2300, where you could get a pizza, a hamburger, or a hot dog and fries.

In spite of all of this, the biggest problem while serving my stint in Korea was boredom in your off-hours. We had a lot of free time on our hands, and boys will be boys. We weren't men yet. We were a bunch of 18- to 22-year-olds from all parts of the United States thrown together in close quarters looking for action to fill up our off-time with. The Army, in all of its wisdom, even tried to solve that problem. At least they thought they did. Every evening seven days a week, the Service Club known as the Jumping I, which was named after the I-Corp Post we were stationed on, was open for business. You could get all of the beer or mixed drinks you wanted—within reason—for 25 cents per drink. For less than $5, you could drink yourself silly and then safely navigate your way back to your barracks. Every night a van, which we called the "meat wagon," would show up at the club full of local girls for our entertainment. You could, if you were so inclined, make an arrangement with these girls to go off the Post for further entertainment.

The Army was not encouraging this sort of activity, but they weren't discouraging it either. They were simply supplying a reason for us all to keep our morale high while we served our time in Korea. You could dance with these girls or you could just talk with them. The only thing you couldn't do was have relations with them on the Post. The Army was doing its part to keep the local economy going. These were "business girls" after all. They had to make a living too. The difference was that these girls carried official medical documentation that they were free of diseases of any kind and were out for a good time too. They all carried "VD cards" guaranteeing that they were fine, upstanding girls. Every month they were required to have medical examinations in order to keep the G.I.'s healthy all-American boys. We had our jobs to do, and we were expected to be at those jobs Monday through Friday during duty time.

However, in spite of all of the Army's efforts, we G.I.'s often found that simply going off the Post to the "Ville," as we called it, provided a more exotic flavor to our activities. There was the risk factor of the unknown. You could get into all kinds of trouble out there. Besides, you could get better bargains off the Post than on it. Money was at a premium for us because we weren't paid very much. So you had to make your money last all month. The girls that came on the Post were fun to be around, but since they were required to receive frequent medical exams they were more expensive dates. They expected you to spend more money on them because they were higher-class girls. The same generally applied at home in the United States. If you wanted to date a rich girl, you had better be prepared to spend some money on her.

In any case, my first venture into the Ville came exactly four days after my arrival at Camp Red Cloud. After finishing my processing-in during the day and going to the paymaster for my wages, I was ready for some entertainment. After dinner at the Mess Hall, I then went to the Jumping I for the evening. While I was there I became a member of the club, which allowed you to set up a credit line when you were short of funds. I met up with a couple of guys who I had met earlier in the day, and I had a great time talking about a little bit of everything with them.

By around 2200, I had a pretty good buzz going and was in very little pain. After returning to the barracks, some of the guys decided that this would be a good time to introduce me to the Ville. Being the lowly Private that I was, I was open at anytime to suggestions from superior-ranked personnel. These guys were SP/5's and SP/4's. I was confident that they would protect me from making a fool out of myself when dealing with the local customs and so forth. As it turned out, they did indeed keep me out of trouble and we returned to the Post unscathed before curfew. I did decide after my first venture into the unknown that I was in need of a camera to fully appreciate the local scenery though.

In an attempt to keep this story in a chronological pattern, I'm going to step back a moment. I had arrived at my permanent duty station for the next 13 months on August 13, 1971. I spent the Friday when I arrived partially processing-in at the various departments in the Battalion offices, and I continued that process the following Monday. By Monday afternoon on the 16th of August, I began my training to become a mail clerk. For the next two weeks I worked with the outgoing mail clerk to learn the job. At the same time, I began studying for the Civil Service Exam that was required of all people handling mail, military or otherwise. Since I was fresh out of college, I had expected to pass this test easily and then settle down into a cushy Army job for the next year or so. However, by August 30th, 1971, I had failed to pass the test once and I was preparing to try again. The test was harder than I thought and it required memorization of postal regulations up the ying yang. I don't know whether it was all the diversions in my off-time or just plain lack of concentration on my part, but I was really struggling to make it as a mail clerk.

One event that happened on the 23rd of August affected my concentration quite a bit. That afternoon, 16 suspected infiltrators from North Korea were killed down in Seoul. There were another five still running around on the loose. There were rumors that there were others near one of our TACH sites near the DMZ, as well as near our OC-71 Radar Command Center. Two-and-a-half ton trucks full of armed Army personnel were sent out from I-Corp to defend our installations and to check out the rumors. In addition to all of this, there were rumors that several North Korean planes crossed the DMZ and went back without being fired on by our HAWK Missile Batteries.

Now this was pretty hairy stuff! While we never went on an official alert, I got the sense that this Army stuff was not all fun and games. Here I was in Bum-Fuck, Korea, and these North Korean clowns were trying to start the Korean Conflict all over again! While most of the guys who had been in the country for a while were laughing and joking around about this, I personally found no humor in any of it. I'll admit that I was scared shitless! I didn't mind doing my duty to God and country, but getting killed or shot at was not my cup of tea. Besides, my weapon of choice was a typewriter, not an M-16 assault rifle. My odds of survival in a real fire fight were marginal at best.

A couple of other things occurred during those two weeks that added to my anxiety. One day while I was working with the outgoing mail clerk, the Command Sergeant Major of the Battalion came by the mailroom. I must explain at this point that for a Private to be conversing with the Sergeant Major usually meant that you had really messed up and had gotten into serious trouble over something. But he simply told me that if anybody came around the mailroom and asked me what I was doing for a job in the Battery I was to tell him that I was the Public Information Clerk in addition to my duties as the mail clerk. He then left without any further explanation. I looked at my friend the mail clerk and asked him what that was all about. He simply shrugged his shoulders and said that he didn't know anything about it. But I could tell by the look in his eyes that he knew something. After pressing him a little on the matter, he admitted that he had been talking to a friend of his down in Personnel at 38th Brigade Headquarters about me. Apparently, he had mentioned that he had a guy in training to replace him who had a degree in journalism.

The 38th Brigade published a newspaper called *The Gauntlet*. Being a new guy in Korea, I was unaware of this fact. It seemed that after finding out about me, Brigade was sending a couple of people up to Camp Red Cloud to try to talk me into transferring down to Brigade to work on the newspaper staff. I guess Brigade didn't have too many people with degrees in journalism on their rosters and they were really interested in employing my writing skills for the newspaper. At the same time, I guess our local Personnel people at 2nd, 71st, ADA had pulled some strings to get me into the Battalion, and they were attempting to hide me from Brigade by giving me additional duties.

The two guys from Brigade showed up a day or two later, and offered to get me transferred down to Osan to work for the newspaper. They were very enthusiastic and made it clear to me that they really wanted me to transfer to Brigade. I was really in a quandary over all of this because I had been at Camp Red Cloud for about three weeks and I had made friends with some of the guys there. I was finally getting comfortable with my surroundings. I wasn't sure that I was ready to pull up stakes and move again.

Their offer was very generous, and I was honored by their request for my services. But I decided that I was ready to settle down and finish my 13 months without any more hassles. I decided to stay at Camp Red Cloud, but I agreed to submit stories on a regular basis to *The Gauntlet* about the activities in our Battalion. I also agreed to write stories for any assignments that the Brigade would come up with in the future. As I will relate later in this story, this decision worked out even better than I would have imagined during the rest of my time in Korea.

The other thing that happened in those two weeks was that through my frequent trips to the Ville I had managed to get a girlfriend. This turned out to be a minor disaster. I negotiated a one-month cohabitation arrangement, which meant that I could come and go as I pleased. I could basically live off the Post only at night when I felt like it. It was a very loose arrangement. This also provided me with great insight into how the general population in Korea lived, such as what they did on a daily basis, where they shopped, and so forth. When you were out in the Ville, you would often go to the local movie house or the local market.

I unfortunately found out that my girlfriend was beautiful but less-than-honorable. She had stolen my Ration Card for the PX and intended to use it for herself. Needless to say, I was extremely pissed-off about this. After receiving some advice from my newfound friends in the Battery, I got the card back from her and vowed not to make that mistake again.

On the morning of August 30th, I was informed by my buddy the mail clerk that I had to go see the First Sergeant before I started work. I was thinking, "Now what did I do wrong?" To my surprise, things were about to change for the better in my short Army career.

CHAPTER TWELVE:

Promotion to PFC: You Are Now the Training and Orientation NCO, the Battalion Public Information Clerk, and a Part-Time Orderly Room Clerk for HQ Battery, 2nd,71st, ADA

Upon arriving at the Orderly Room on the morning of August 30th, 1971, the First Sergeant informed me that from that day forward I was the new Training and Orientation NCO for HQ Battery. In addition, I was to continue as the Battalion Public Information Clerk in my spare time, and I would also be training to take over the Morning Report Clerk's job. It seemed that the Army had finally recognized that I could type 50 words per minute and put two sentences together and have them make sense. The plan became very obvious. I was eventually going to be the sole HQ Battery clerk within the next few months. The First Sergeant didn't tell me that at the time, but that is how it would turn out in the end.

To add to the excitement of that day, our outgoing Battalion Commander decided to call an alert drill for HQ Battery. This called for everyone in the Battery to show up in formation with full field gear on and weapons in hand. This whole affair ended up being more like a Chinese Fire Drill because it was a totally confusing activity. Everyone was running around grabbing their field gear that they normally never even looked at, more or less used. They were running to the Armory and getting their weapons that they never used, and then they finally stood rank and file in formation for the arrival of the Battalion Commander so that he could inspect us for our combat preparedness.

The whole affair took about an hour to an hour-and-a-half. The First Sergeant wrote down all of our names on a clipboard so the officers could determine who had made it and who didn't. After standing around and generally goofing-off for another 15 minutes, the Battalion Commander finally arrived to review the troops. He walked down the lines of the formation checking out our haircuts, lengthy mustaches, and sloppy uniforms. He even jumped on a couple of guys for being overweight. Several guys got it for not coming to full attention when he came by them. Fortunately, I managed to avoid any criticism. I came to the conclusion while I was standing there in formation that if it had been a real alert, the North Koreans could have helped us put our field gear on by the time we got it together.

By the 2nd of September, I was hard at work learning my new duties as Training and Orientation NCO and part-time Orderly Room Clerk. The first few days were very confusing and I had no idea what I was doing, but as time went on my typing skills returned to me and I actually started figuring out how to do the Morning Report. At first it took me several hours to do this report because it was done on stencils for permanent recording purposes and to make copies from. If you made a typing error on these or spelled somebody's name wrong you had to start all over again. By the time I left Korea I became quite proficient at doing this report. By then I was cranking it out in less than two hours, leaving the rest of the day for other reports and letters that needed to be typed.

At about this same time, I received my first care package from home. My parents sent me a real nice sweater that I could wear in my downtime, along with several goodies including a canned ham, a popcorn popper, candy bars, and other assorted snacks. For years, my family and I had a private joke about the starving kids in Korea. As a kid, whenever I didn't want to finish my meals my parents would remind me that there were starving kids in Korea and that I should eat my food because I was fortunate to have it. I found out that there were no starving kids in Korea.

They were living in conditions less fortunate than we had in the United States, but they were certainly not starving. I made this point quite clear to my parents in the several letters that I sent to them.

I continued learning my new job over the next couple of weeks, and I started to get into a groove working in the Orderly Room. I celebrated my 23rd birthday on September 13, 1971. My birthday present was getting a promotion to Private First Class. There was an official pinning ceremony put on by the First Sergeant. Part of this ceremony included everyone in the Orderly Room punching you in the arms to congratulate you on being promoted. I didn't mind all of this abuse because I was getting a pay raise. Money in Korea was always a problem. No matter how diligent you were about spreading it out over a month, it always seemed that you were broke several days ahead of payday.

My reverie over my promotion to PFC ended abruptly at 0500 the very next morning. The alert siren was going off again. There we were again, running around like fools trying to get our shit together and show up for formation. We did a little better this time. We were all in formation in front of the Battalion offices by 0600. This was quite remarkable considering that some of us had come from the Ville to get there. Our much-loved outgoing Battalion Commander was there giving people shit for one thing or another. As I was standing in formation, the First Sergeant came up to me and said "Poindexter, what are you doing here?" I replied, "Isn't this where I am supposed to be?" He answered that from now on when we had these alerts, I was supposed to go straight to the Orderly Room, put on a pot of coffee, and answer the phone if somebody called.

The First Sergeant's orders made perfect sense to me, so off to the Orderly Room I went. I put on a pot of coffee and waited for the phone to ring, which never happened. About 45 minutes later, the First Sergeant and the Battery Commander arrived at the Orderly Room and invited me to breakfast. Here I was a lowly PFC, and I was going to breakfast with the Battery Commander and the First Sergeant. This was not a normal occurrence. I usually ate my meals with the other non-coms (non-officers and Staff Sergeants) separately in the Battery. While we ate, the two of them explained how critical my duties were when these alerts took place. Making coffee and answering the phone were extremely important because everyone else was too busy mustering up the troops. These revelations made perfect sense to me. I took a lot of ribbing from my friends later on that day about having breakfast with the bosses. They all accused me of sucking-up for future perks. I of course pleaded complete innocence in the whole matter. I had to admit though that it was a pretty cool event.

On the following day, we started practicing marching in formation for the Battalion Commander's Change of Command Ceremony. Since we all just loved the present Battalion Commander, we drilled very hard to perfect our marching. After about a week of practice we managed to get fairly proficient in our techniques. We even looked pretty good, considering some of us hadn't done any serious marching since Basic Training. We were ready for the Change of Command Ceremony.

The day before the ceremony was to take place, I got my first taste of handling things by myself in the Orderly Room. By 0800, I became "Command PFC" of HQ Battery, 2nd, 71st, ADA. The First Sergeant and the other clerk in the Orderly Room were off to ASCOM in Seoul to check on incoming personnel for the Battery. The Battery Commander was running around the Battalion offices and parade grounds in preparation for the Change of Command Ceremony for our out-going and incoming Battalion Commander. This left me in charge of the Orderly Room. It was a little hectic answering the phone, doing the Morning Report, and taking care of everything else that was going on in the Battery. I was getting a taste of the future though. I was to find out that in a few short months I would be the only clerk in the Orderly Room.

The big ceremony took place the next day. It was quite a production number. We paraded past the new and old Battalion Commanders and other dignitaries, including several Generals from Brigade Headquarters. We were in our dress uniforms, red scarves and all. We also had to carry our seldom-used M-16 rifles. We even had the Brigade Band in place for the ceremony. We basically goofed-off for the rest of the day. We had to stick around because the Brigade Commander stayed at Camp Red Cloud until 1500 hours.

As I mentioned earlier, part of my duties in the Orderly Room included taking over as the Training and Orientation NCO. Whenever we received replacement personnel at HQ Battery, as well as when men were going to our Battalion's other Batteries, it was my job to orientate them regarding

110

the do's and don'ts of their tour in Korea. It apparently was determined that since I had been in Korea for a month that I was now an expert in the ways of proper behavior when not at work. So as each new replacement came into the Battery, I went over the various subjects such as contact with the opposite sex, where to go, where not to go, what to do if you contracted VD from some friend in the Ville, and so forth. I gave them the speech about how to avoid trouble with the Korean civilian authorities. I also had to set up training schedules for the rifle range so that everyone would stay current on their qualifications on the use of their M-16's and other weapons.

As for my Public Information Clerk duties, I began submitting stories to *The Gauntlet* newspaper. I wrote stories about activities at HQ Battery, including a big story on our recent Change of Command Ceremony. I was kept pretty busy with all of these duties. By the end of September, I was settling in as a full-time member of the Orderly Room staff.

CHAPTER THIRTEEN:

Turkish Baths, Football Games, Cooler Weather, and Dwindling Relationships at Home

October rolled in and I was an integral part of the Orderly Room. I was again playing the role of Command PFC since my fellow clerk was off to ASCOM. This time he was escorting a 212 to ASCOM so he could send him out of the country and back to the United States for his formal removal from the U.S. Army. The individual, a Vietnam veteran, was leaving on a general discharge for going AWOL too many times while on active duty. The Battery Commander and my fellow clerk in the Orderly Room went to the Stockade (the Army's version of a detention center or jail) and picked up this guy. They then drove to Seoul to ship him out.

This G.I. had been in the Stockade for 60 days waiting for the Army, in all of its efficiency, to get things arranged for him to leave the country. Why it took the Army 60 days to get a few documents together, I'll never know. In any case, you can imagine what a great mood this guy was in after 60 days of confinement. Both the Battery Commander and my clerk buddy were carrying 45's when they left the Orderly Room to go get him. It was kind of scary to think about it. I mean after all, here was a guy who had fought in Vietnam and had received the Bronze Star for valor under fire. Now he was leaving the Army under less-than-desirable circumstances.

You couldn't tell what this guy was going to do at any given moment. I was thinking that this was one duty I would not enjoy if I was called upon to escort somebody somewhere.

A couple of friends and I decided to try out some of the local and more exotic places in Uijongbu. Since we had just gotten paid we for once had money to play with and time to burn. It was decided by democratic vote that we should investigate the infamous Onasis Hotel. We were battered and bruised after playing football in the morning against a team made up of the Battery's officers. For some reason, they were in better shape than we were. We lost the game on a disputed field goal by our new Battery Commander. I did score a touchdown during the game so I wasn't completely deflated by the outcome. After an afternoon siesta and licking our wounds for a while, we prepared for our assault on downtown Uijongbu.

The Onasis Hotel was known for both its hospitality to G.I.'s and its Turkish baths. There was a bevy of attractive young ladies in the bar, and we were amazed to find out that they were all experts in the art of Turkish bathing. We all made our arrangements with the local talent, and before I knew it I was escorted to a room by my date for the night. She was a stunning girl with long legs and very few clothes on. After getting comfortable with her and my accommodations, she indicated that we should get ready to take a bath together in the hot tub in the next room. She had me remove my clothes and get into the tub. She was very encouraging and did a lot of giggling along the way. I am not sure what she was giggling about. It was either my hairy body, my lack of size in certain areas, or my complete naivete to this whole situation. After all, I wasn't used to taking baths with someone watching! To make matters even more complex, once I was in the tub and comfortable she then removed what little clothing she had on and stepped in the tub with me. Now this is the kind of stuff that most guys dream about. Here I was in a tub with an attractive young lady proceeding to wash me from head to toe. She even inspected me for lice all over everywhere. I couldn't believe what was happening to me.

After bathing, receiving a complete body massage, and much personal attention from my lovely date, I was very much invigorated. We had a late romantic dinner, in the nude of course, and settled in for the night. The next morning my buddies and I left the hotel in great spirits and a little lighter in the pocketbook. We all agreed that we would have to visit this place again in the future. Keeping one's morale up, after all, was a major priority during our time in Korea. We were obligated to do this. The Army thought that sheer work and lots of physical activity was the answer to everything. After our experience at the Onasis Hotel, we all agreed that this was a much more sensible way to keep our spirits up during our stay in Korea. I from this point forward included this recommendation in my orientation program.

Monday, October 1, 1971 marked the first day that I needed to wear my field jacket since arriving in Korea. Korean weather was another one of the adjustments that I had to get used to. In the summer months it was very hot and muggy and is similar to many places down south in the United States. Then the monsoon season begins in August. I had arrived in Korea just in time for the monsoon season. It rained almost every day. You were either wet from the humidity or from the torrential downpours all the time.

The Army at Camp Red Cloud had a unique method for running off all of this water. Extending throughout the length and breadth of Camp Red Cloud were cement drainage ditches. These ditches were about 2- to 3-feet deep and would literally fill up with running water during the monsoons. When it stopped raining for a few hours the strangest phenomena occurred. These same ditches filled up with thousands of tiny frogs. There were so many of them that they would overflow the ditches and get out in the grass and on the sidewalks. It was hard to walk anywhere without stepping on them. Sometimes they would even get into the buildings. I remember waking up one morning and finding one looking down at me from the other side of the mosquito netting that was covering my bed. I thought I was having a nightmare or something.

The fun part came that winter. Korean winters were a lot harsher than I was used to back in Chicago. It would get consistently below zero, and the wind was always there blowing off the mountains that surrounded our Post. When it snowed those drainage ditches would fill up and suddenly become invisible. Every so often, someone would be walking along and suddenly drop into the ditch into waist-deep snow. We got a lot of laughs out of these events. In fact, that was one of our ongoing jokes in the

Battery. We wouldn't tell the new guys about the ditches, and we took bets on how long it would take for one of them to fall into one on a snowy day. I admit it was a little sadistic, but we were always looking for new diversions from our daily routine.

While I was in Korea I stayed in touch with a couple of girlfriends back in Illinois. We wrote letters back and forth for a while, but as time went on the principle of "out of sight, out of mind" eventually took over our letter-writing enthusiasm. I had been pretty serious with one girl during my days at Northern Illinois University. But as my luck would have it, her boyfriend came back from Vietnam and I was kind of out of the picture. She did continue to write to me for a couple of months, but all she ever wrote about was her engagement to this guy and their plans for their upcoming wedding. After a while I suggested in one of my letters that I saw no point in continuing to write back and forth since it was obvious that we had no future other than being friends. The same applied to the other girl in my life. She wrote to me very infrequently and I got the impression that she would not be waiting for me at the airport when I returned to Illinois. Therefore, we just gradually quit writing after a few letters. Besides, I had the Ville to go to with all of its short girls with their beautiful legs and friendly attitudes. I didn't plan on falling in love in Korea, but it sure was fun falling in lust for 13 months.

CHAPTER FOURTEEN:

Officially the Morning Report Clerk, No Hot Water, More Football, Transients, and Part-Time Building Inspector

I officially became the Morning Report Clerk on the 5th of October. I was even given a new electric typewriter to work with. As I have mentioned, these morning reports were a status report that accounted for all personnel in the Battery. You had to record the number of people who were sick, on leave, temporarily detached to other units, those leaving and arriving, those in training, and so forth. We used stencils for these reports, and then we ran off copies for all of the departments that the report had to be sent to.

You had to make several phone calls to verify that all of the information going in the report was correct. I did this report daily first thing in the morning, which is how it got its name. The First Sergeant had great confidence in me. I think he realized very early that I could type pretty fast without too many mistakes. The second time I did this report, however, I was sailing along only to discover two pages into it that I had left the carbons out! I had to start all over again, taking me most of the day to complete it. Oh well, the Army had lots of morning report forms. I became very proficient at this as time went on. The only problem with this was that the sooner you finished it, the more stuff the First Sergeant gave you to do. The whole trick was to look busy without doing any work. I got pretty good at that too.

As I mentioned earlier, cooler weather was on its way. Now you would think that the Army would make sure that all of the plumbing in the buildings was up to par for the cold Korean winter months. I mean after all, it gets really cold every winter. The first thing that happened was that we started out without any hot water. The guys in our barracks started complaining right away. Day after day, we started our days with cold showers. This went on for several days before someone was sent to fix the problem. Maybe there was a shortage of plumbers in Korea. Who knows?

After about a week the situation improved, and three guys could get a hot shower before the hot water ran out. It never improved beyond that. So began the great shower races for the rest of the time I was in Korea. Every morning it was the same thing. Everyone was hurrying to get into the shower first before the hot water ran out. Now this was usually a friendly competition, but as you might expect after a while it wasn't funny anymore. There was a lot of jostling around for position, and the thought of sharing the hot water coming out of three showerheads for 20-some guys never occurred to anyone.

October 10th marked the day of the big football game with Alpha Battery. Our two local football teams combined forces to take on the "Neanderthals" from Alpha Battery. The rumor was that these guys were really tough and took their football very seriously. The Neanderthals showed up in two-and-a-half-ton trucks with 35 to 40 guys in all. HQ Battery barely managed to field a team at all. We had just enough guys to play the game with all of us playing both ways—offense and defense. Needless to say, we were completely outmatched. Alpha Battery went up 24-0 in the first half. After our Battery Commander took over at quarterback we faired a little better, making the final score a lot closer than we had expected. We lost 30-22. Yours truly, Mr. Butterfingers, failed to catch a single pass all day. I did pretty well on defense and made a few good blocks in our efforts to make a comeback. Considering I was a whopping 130 pounds at the time, I thought I did pretty well against the big guys.

A few days later, we were overrun by new replacements just arriving into the country. Sixteen new people came in on the first day, followed by 25 more the following day. I, of course, gave them their orientation speech and then escorted them through the other sections in the Battalion offices. For two days I had a lot of fun snowing my buddies working in these sections. They were buried in typing forms for each new guy, and I was enjoying the hell out of bringing them more and more work. My fun with all of this ended on the afternoon of the second day, however.

On that day, after work I went to the barracks only to find transients throughout our building. Since we didn't have extra quarters for all of these guys we had to billet them with us overnight before shipping them out to their permanent duty stations. I had to share my cube with a guy who was in need of a bath in the worst way. I left the window open partway to keep from gagging on the smell. I did suggest to him that we indeed had showers, but he never quite got the message. In a way I felt sorry for him. He was having a hell of a time adjusting to things. Since he was leaving in the morning no one had really given him the time of day, and he had no idea where anything was on the Post. I made sure that he at least found the Mess Hall.

A lot of these new guys came from Fort Bliss where I did my AIT. After talking to several of them, I found out that they had been screwed by my favorite D.I. Sugar Bear. He apparently took great pleasure in messing with people and seeing that they didn't get promoted out of AIT. This fact would come back to haunt him later in this story. He eventually rotated into Korea before I left, and I made sure he was warmly welcomed to his new duty station. More on this later.

Right in the middle of all of this mayhem with the incoming replacement people was when the Battery Commander sent me on a very strange mission. He told me that he needed me to go to the other buildings in our compound and count and measure all of the windows. He explained that he needed all of this information so he could order new material for curtains. I thought this to be rather strange since the Army was notorious for using things until they were completely worn out. After all, the buildings in our compound dated back to the Korean Conflict. While they were adequate to live and work in they were nothing to write home about. Why we needed new curtains I'll never know. In spite of my questioning the sanity of this request, I proceeded to follow his instructions.

As you might imagine, as I went through the different buildings and offices counting and measuring windows I took a lot of crap from my fellow clerks. They got quite a kick out of my assigned task. They suggested that maybe I was failing as the Morning Report Clerk so the Battery Commander was giving me other duties more suited to my intelligence. They even suggested that I could do this job better if I was wearing a skirt! I took all of this razzing in good spirits since I had had my fun in the previous few days snowing them with work.

CHAPTER FIFTEEN:

Pre-Holiday Blues, PT Tests, M-16 Familiarization, Basketball, and a Cast of Characters

The rest of October rolled by without a lot of action and very little mail from home. As each day went by without mail, I was slowly becoming depressed and I was not too excited about spending the holidays away from home. My work in the Orderly Room was progressing slowly with many ups and downs. I was really sinking into the "G.I. blues." I realized that I had a long time to go in Korea, and the thought of how many days I had left was enough to make me throw up. It took all of my willpower on most days to get up to do my duties. The weather was deteriorating toward winter, and our hot water situation in the barracks was not improving. Life in Korea really sucked.

There were a few highlights during this time though. My friends and I went to a USO show at the Service Club. It featured the play "A Funny Thing Happened on the Way to the Forum." The show was hilarious and was by far the best production we had seen since arriving in Korea. There was something different this time—there were American girls in the play. For us sex-starved G.I.'s, this was really a treat! They were all cute and very pleasing to watch. I think they all probably had a lot of talent but we really didn't notice. We were too busy looking at them in their skimpy Roman togas!

I had to take my fifth PT test in the last eight months of my Army career on the 21ˢᵗ of October. Apparently, my physical condition had deteriorated since my last PT test at Fort Bliss in spite of playing football on a regular basis for the past month or so. I complained wholeheartedly about having to go through all of this again, but I had to take the test anyway. The Army had its regulations. I passed the test with flying colors once again. After completing the test, I then had to go out to the North Star Rifle Range and re-familiarize myself with my unused M-16. I shot off about 10 rounds of ammunition, which I thought was a complete waste of time since I had no intention of ever having to fire my weapon again.

Card-playing was a regular activity in our off-time back then. I have always been a pretty decent card player, and I was fairly proficient at most card games such as poker, Canasta, Hearts, and Spades back then. Most of us attempted to augment our meager salaries with money earned in these card games. However, lately I had been losing my ass! Between my card-playing losses and my severe lack of mail, I was going through a terrible time.

At the end of the month, the Battery Commander announced that HQ Battery was going to field a team for the upcoming basketball season. Since I was going through such a bad streak of luck at card-playing I decided to get involved in another activity. Being a rather height-challenged individual at 5'5 ½" or so, basketball was never one of my better sports. I had played for church leagues and intramural leagues in high school as well as a few college pick-up games, but basketball was never my game. Undaunted, I showed up for practice and originally made the team due to a lack of interest by other guys in the Battery. We had about 10 or so guys who went out for the team.

The first league game was scheduled for November 5ᵗʰ. From what I saw at the first few practices we had a lot of work to do. Our team really sucked at basketball. We had a couple of guys who were pretty good, but for the most part we were lousy. This did not bode well for the upcoming season. After a couple of practice games with our DSP unit, we actually began to gel as a team and looked competitive, if nothing else. My playing time was very limited for obvious reasons. But it was something to do in the evenings and on the weekends. We never got past the first round in any of the tournaments we played in. My lack of playing time caused me at one point to quit in favor of a much taller guy for the good of the team. However, I later joined the team when an extra uniform became available. Lack of participants on the team was a constant problem for HQ Battery. The sheer lack of active players got me more playing time as the season wore on, and I actually scored a few points much to the delight of my teammates.

By the first week of November, I had managed to catch my first cold since arriving in Korea. I probably caught it during my frequent visits to the Ville. Catching things down in the Ville was quite common. Some guys caught VD from unclean girls. I was gratified to know that all I caught was a cold. I started spending a lot of my off-duty time in the barracks reading. Several days went by without any cigarettes or booze while I recovered from my cold. This fact was significant because being only eight miles from the DMZ, drinking and smoking to steady your nerves were regular activities at Camp Red Cloud.

On November 16th, the First Sergeant informed me that I had been recommended for "Soldier of the Quarter" due to my diligent work in the Orderly Room. I really wasn't feeling that dedicated to my military standing, but the powers-that-be thought I was deserving. I guess it was my good work ethic taught to me by my parents when I was a kid. At least I showed up for work every Monday morning. My morning report skills were improving but were nothing to write home about. My only real goal was to get out of Korea and the sooner the better. Anyway, I had to start studying so I could go before a board of NCO's in order to receive this award. Among other things, I had to memorize certain facts about the Army and its history. There were oaths that had to be recited and so forth. We were then interviewed by a board of Staff Sergeants in regard to what we did above and beyond the normal call of duty. My roles as the Battalion Public Information NCO, my writing for *The Gauntlet* newspaper, and serving as the Orientation NCO for the Battery played into my being nominated for the award.

My friends and I participated in a few off-duty fun activities during the week leading up to Thanksgiving. We went to a "powder-puff" football game in Seoul. The players were female high school students from a school in Korea. One of the players, a cute little blonde wearing #34 (Walter Payton's number) must have been on something though. She waved her arms up and down attempting to do what looked like flying every time she ran onto or off the field. We razzed her all afternoon from the top row of the grandstand. We spent the whole time trying to get these girls to pose for pictures, but none of them were the slightest bit interested. You would have thought that all of these older men watching them play would have been a thrill for them. I guess not.

The Service Club offered many activities. We played Bingo on a regular basis. We also watched many American movies. We got the chance to watch the Nebraska-Oklahoma football game via satellite the day after Thanksgiving after having our fill of turkey at the Mess Hall. We had to get up at 0500 to watch the game, but it was well worth it. If you thought about it, we really didn't have it too bad in Korea. The Army did make an effort to make us feel comfortable and provided us with many amenities.

I encountered many strange and interesting people during my stay in Korea. Many of these guys became close friends of mine. They formed a very diverse group of G.I.'s from every part of the United States. At this point in my story, I would like to share with you some of my observations of these guys.

One individual comes immediately to mind. He was a truck driver and a mechanic for the Battery. Normally while he was on duty, this guy was a pretty good guy and he did his job quite well. He was almost a model soldier. However, once he was off-duty he changed from Dr. Jekyll to Mr. Hyde. He had a penchant for getting into trouble, especially down in the Ville. It seemed that every time he went off the Post, which was practically every night, he got drunk and started messing around with the girls and the Mamasans.

Each time he returned just before curfew, and he often came back with battle scars. These included black eyes, bruises, and scrapes. He would come into the barracks raising all kinds of hell. He would yell at the top of his lungs, waking up everyone in the building. One night he was so drunk and upset that he somehow tore off one of the sinks in the bathroom. He caught holy hell for that move the next day. Our attempts to calm him down in these situations were a waste of time. We gradually decided to just leave him alone when he came in like that. He was obviously an alcoholic, and he maybe had some other problems to boot.

Another guy was from back east somewhere. I remember when he came into Korea because when I gave him my orientation speech about staying out of trouble, he must have either not been paying attention or he forgot what I said to him the minute he walked out the door. He came in once a month for a pass to the infirmary to get a shot so he could get rid of his VD. This went on for as long as I was in Korea. After a few times I was curious, so I asked if he was seeing the same girl all the time. He said that he had a girlfriend in the Ville and that he was thinking about marrying her and taking her back to the States. He couldn't understand why he couldn't get rid of the clap though. I suggested that maybe his girlfriend was infected and she kept giving it to him. He, of course, would not listen to this logic.

There were other guys who simply walked around with permanent smiles on their faces. I knew that it wasn't because they were thrilled to be stationed in Korea. As I mentioned earlier, you could literally get anything 50 yards outside of the gates of Camp Red Cloud. This included marijuana and other drugs. There were many of my comrades who took advantage of this on a regular basis. I, being a conservative red-blooded American boy, stayed away from this stuff.

Most of the guys I worked with in the Battery and Battalion offices were pretty straight guys. Since we were all college graduates, we found other more intellectual pursuits to occupy our off-time with. Once in a while we fell off the wagon and ran amuck in the Ville, but for the most part we stayed out of trouble by staying on the Post and making use of the facilities and activities that were provided for us by the Army. Some of us even used the library and the Chapel every so often.

There were a few smart-asses in the group, as you might expect. These were the guys who made fun of everybody else but didn't like it when you turned the tables and made fun of them. After many months in close proximity to each other, sometimes our personalities clashed and arguments would occur. But for the most part, we all got along fairly well. We all had our jobs to do, and the jobs required us to communicate with each other almost every day. Being pissed-off at somebody for very long just didn't make any sense.

CHAPTER SIXTEEN:

Soldier of the Quarter Board, The 20-Day War, The Popcorn Popper Meal, and Christmas in Korea

On December 2, I went before the Soldier of the Quarter Board. The Board was made up of the Command Sergeant Major and the five First Sergeants from the Batteries in the Battalion. There were five of us up for the award—one from each Battery. After the candidates were interviewed by the Board, a vote was taken to determine who won the award. I unfortunately came in second in the balloting. My First Sergeant told me that I had done just fine in the interview and that it had been a very close vote, 3-2. Besides, if I had won the award the rest of the Batteries would probably have cried foul since I was so close in my work with the CSM and the First Sergeant. I was satisfied that my boss was happy with me. That was all that really mattered.

December 7, 1971, which marked the 30th anniversary of the attack on Pearl Harbor by the Japanese, was an interesting day for me. First of all, the Brigade Commander from Osan came for a visit to our facility. We had known ahead of time that he was coming, so we had spent several days prior preparing for his arrival. Everything in the Battery buildings was cleaned and shined. All of the walls received a new coat of paint, and all of the floors were stripped of their old wax and a new fresh coat of wax was applied. We even put up new curtains on the windows. It was quite a performance.

I still had my regular duties to perform in between all of this activity. In typical Army fashion, this time was chosen to send over 30 new arrivals in Korea through our Battery for processing and assignment to other Batteries. I had to add all of these people to our roster and morning reports, and then as they left on their assignments, I had to remove them again. This was very tedious work and it required several hours every day to perform. At around this same time, there were some serious situations going on in Korea. There were many political protests occurring throughout the country. There was a rumor going around that a 20-day war between North Korea and South Korea was about to take place. The South Korean Army was on high alert for several days. We at Camp Red Cloud were expecting an alert at any time. Everyone was busy getting all of their stuff in order just in case.

In reality the houseboys were doing all of this, but nobody was questioning our dedication and patriotism. Houseboys were like our mother-away-from-home. They washed our clothes and ironed them so that we were always in tiptop shape uniform-wise. They made our beds and kept our barracks in an orderly fashion. They also kept our lockers and so forth in perfect condition in case there was an inspection by the Battery officers. We basically didn't do anything for ourselves other than getting up every morning and caring for our own personal hygiene. And the houseboys did all of this for the bargain price of $10 per month. Each houseboy had about six guys assigned to him. Believe it or not, this was a lot of money for them at the time.

As for the alerts, our uniforms and other field gear were in our lockers in the barracks. Any time there was an alert, we had to gather all of this gear and carry it down to the formation just in case we were required to actually go out on maneuvers or possibly go into actual battle. Our weapons were kept in the Armory, but the rest of our gear was in our lockers. The houseboys kept all of this in order for us even though it was really our job.

Most of us joked around about these alerts to ease the tension. However, in the back of everyone's mind was the thought, "What if this is the real thing? Did we really want to get into a real fight with live ammo and all that?" I, for one, had no interest in that at all. I was perfectly happy doing my paperwork. Besides, I had proved in Basic Training that I couldn't shoot worth a damn! With my luck I'd get shot right off the bat, ending my otherwise brilliant Army career.

About a week before Christmas 1971, which was my first Christmas spent out of the good old United States, things were settling down on the political front in Korea. It was back to the same old routine every day. We did have ping-pong and pool tournaments at HQ Battery though. My friends and I spent a lot of time at the NCO Club practicing our skills. On December 19th, we spent the entire morning playing pool. Then from about 1 in the afternoon until about 6 in the evening, we played Canasta. We were having such a great time that we forgot about dinner. Since we were too late for the Mess Hall meal, we all decided to pool our resources from our care packages that had recently arrived from home.

I brought out my popcorn popper to cook my treasures from home. These treasures included a small canned ham, two bags of Ramen noodles, a couple of hard-boiled eggs from the Mess Hall from breakfast (we were allowed to take things back to the barracks for a future snack during the day), and a can of vegetable soup. We had a six-pack of Coke to go with this gourmet meal. This worked out so well that we did this several more times in Korea. It took a while to heat all of the ingredients, but it was well worth the wait in the end. It did prove one thing: When you are hungry enough you will eat just about anything!

Christmas arrived in Korea. It was a very strange feeling for me to not be at home with my parents and family. I am not sure that I really missed everyone that much since it was my first Christmas away on my own. It was just different I guess. I received a very nice care package from home with all kinds of good stuff to munch on. I even received some extra civilian clothes to wear in my off-time. These kinds of things were at a premium in Korea. After all, you couldn't just run down to the local Sears or Penney's store to buy clothes. Everything had to be bought at the PX or down in the Ville. It was actually easier for me to find clothes in the Ville. There were a lot of short people in Korea.

We went to half-day work schedules during the holidays. This left us with a lot of free time on our hands. The First Sergeant was gone for 30 days in Alaska on leave, so I was on my own to run the Orderly Room. It was about this time that the Army started its Early-Out Program. Due to less money from Congress, the Army started cutting down the amount of time you had to serve in the military after being drafted. The war in Vietnam was starting to wind down a little and it appeared that our withdrawal from the country was imminent. Therefore, it was determined that if you were on a hardship tour while in the Army your commitment to the Service would be reduced to 19 months instead of the normal 24-month commitment.

A hardship tour of duty was one in which you could not have your dependents come over and stay with you on your assignment because there were combat or potential combat situations that could arise. The families instead had to stay in the United States. Otherwise, the Army usually provided billeting for soldiers with families on the base at a lower cost than living off the base among the civilian population. Since most of us were young single guys, these situations never really came up anyway. But for some of the guys who made the Army a career such as Staff Sergeants, many of them had families.

It was clear to me that I would be the head honcho in the Orderly Room in the very near future. As it turned out, I ended up being the only honcho in the Orderly Room, but more on this later. As I mentioned, we had a lot of free time on our hands. I failed miserably in both the ping-pong and pool tournaments. I lost to one of the Korean soldiers in the ping-pong tournament, and I lost to an old Sergeant in the pool tournament. So I ended up just watching these tournaments for great lengths of time.

Even my exploits on the HQ Battery basketball team became rather limited. My playing time became nil or none. I wasn't a very good shot, and I was entirely too short to be a big contributor to the team. Besides, the team was not very good in the first place. Our team would go on to fall out of the end-of-season tournament very early with or without me. With a lot of guys leaving the Army due to the Early- Out Program, the team's numbers were dwindling. There were a couple of games where we barely had enough guys show up to field a team.

Since the New Year was quickly arriving in Korea, I began planning my 10-day leave to Japan. Saving money was the hardest thing to do. It took a great amount of discipline to not go out to the Ville or the NCO Club in the evenings after work. I spent a lot of time writing what seemed like one-way letters to friends and relatives back in the States. Waiting on return mail from others was a real drag. I wasn't the best letter-writer in the world, but if I was to take an account of this I probably sent out more letters than I received during my stay in Korea.

By New Year's Eve I was ready for a night out on the town. I must have not done anything exciting since I don't recall anything particular about that evening. I actually didn't even mention it in my journal that I kept while I was in Korea. I think I had a rather subdued New Year's Eve and retired early due to a lack of funds to operate with. Most of my buddies did the same thing for one reason: no money!

CHAPTER SEVENTEEN:

The New Year, Another Promotion, and Japan or Bust!

I spent New Year's Day of 1972 like most Americans: watching football bowl games. The only difference was that due to the International Dateline, our games were broadcast on New Year's evening and into the next day. I remember watching the Orange Bowl at about 3 in the morning on the 2nd of January. It was very strange sitting up all night watching football with a bunch of guys from every part of the United States. There were your usual rivalries among the guys and their favorite teams. I have to give the Army credit here. They tried to make us feel right at home. The Day Room was made available for all of us to watch the games in, and snacks of different sorts were provided. It wasn't quite like home, but it was tolerable.

After a somewhat subdued New Year's holiday, it was back to work in the military. The weeks rolled by without too much exciting going on. Of course there was Mail Call every day, but that was not very exciting. I usually had the same routine: Show up for work, do the morning report, and take care of correspondence and filing. After work it was reading, listening to music, playing cards with friends, or traveling to the NCO Club or the Ville. I usually spent most of my time hanging around in the barracks since I was trying to save money for my upcoming leave to Japan.

One new event did occur though. I got to move to the "high-rent district" of the barracks. With all of the guys leaving through the Early-Out Program, space opened up in the better end of the barracks. I managed to secure a cubicle in the warm end of the building. Winters in Korea are really fierce and cold. The heating in the buildings worked just about as well as the water heaters did for the showers. One end of the building was warm, and the other end was cold all the time. I was very glad to finally get out of the cold end of the building. I was quickly becoming an old head in the Battery.

On the 8th of January, I tried to make a call home to the States, but as luck would have it nobody was home. I then tried to call my brother, Ken, back in Illinois, and I for some reason got the wrong number. It ended up being a complete waste of time, which did nothing to alleviate my boredom. There were rumors of an alert being called that night, but that didn't happen either. I woke up the next morning at around 6:30 to the sound of the Post cannon, which went off every morning of the year at the same time, rain or shine, sleet or snow.

To improve my morale, I came out of "retirement" from basketball and rejoined the team for the balance of the season since an extra uniform became available. My basketball skills were on the same level as before, but it was something to do without spending any money.

I finally got through on a call home and I talked with my mother for about 15 minutes. I told her of my plans to buy stereo equipment while I was in Korea, and I mentioned my upcoming leave to Japan. I had chosen to go to Japan rather than home to Illinois primarily due to a lack of funds and a lack of time. Besides, I had always wanted to see Japan, and since we were already halfway around the world it was convenient. The Winter Olympics were also going on in Sapporo, Japan at the time. My mother was excited to hear from her son, as all mothers would be. My dad was not at home, but the call lifted my spirits quite a bit anyway.

At around this same time, I got a call from my old buddy Heir Rommel. We had been separated since our arrival in Korea. We vowed to stay in touch when we could in the future. He was stationed in Osan in a NIKE-HERCULES surface-to-air missile Battalion. Our prospects for getting together were pretty slim since we were quite a distance from each other, but we did stay in touch by phone from then on until our tours were over in Korea.

On the 19th of January 1972, I took great pleasure in writing and typing my own recommendation for promotion to the rank of SP/4. In just a few short days I was going to be promoted again. It came with more pay and everything else that goes with a promotion. One of my numerous duties was to compile a list every month of those who were eligible for promotion. I also typed up their recommendations. So every time that I became eligible, I naturally made sure my name was on the list in a prominent position so the Battery Commander could not possibly miss it. I always got a lot of grief from him about this, but at the same time I always received the promotion.

About 10 days before my expected departure to go on leave in Japan, I caught another cold and had to nurse myself back to health. It wasn't that easy to run in and out of buildings into sub-freezing weather. But somehow I felt better before I was to leave. That is one of my lasting impressions of military life to this day. I have never had as many colds in my entire life than when I was in the military. Maybe it was the close proximity to a bunch of sometimes unhealthy guys that did it. I have found that the male species does not always fare well in day-to-day living without the presence of the female species. I think that we men have a tendency to stay cleaner and look after ourselves better when women are involved in our lives.

The total lack of girls in the military during those days definitely played a role in why I kept catching these blooming colds. Korea wasn't too sanitary to begin with. Fifty yards off the Post grounds you went from paved sidewalks to mud streets and wall-to-wall garbage pits. The girls who were around in the Ville seemed to be clean and care about their overall health, but we didn't exactly conduct surveys on this. You took one look from the exterior view and that was the extent of the inspection.

One Saturday while I waited for the beginning of my leave to Japan, I had a chance to sit down with my houseboy, Kwan. A couple of my buddies and I used to get into extended conversations with him on occasion. Kwan was really a very bright guy. We learned at some point that he was a trained civil engineer. He explained that he chose to be a houseboy because it paid better than being a civil engineer. This was hard to believe, but true. You could carry on an intelligent conversation with this guy in spite of his limited English vocabulary.

On many of those occasions we talked about the recent tension and political unrest in Korea. According to Kwan, the North Koreans would never come back in force like they did during the Korean Conflict. The reason was that the South Korean Army was so built-up by the Americans that they were better-trained and better-armed than the North Koreans. He also explained that the South Koreans were much like the Israelis in their resolve to be independent from North Korea. In spite of all the political unrest and tension, the South Korean people were very much on the same page when it came to keeping the North Koreans in their place. The bottom line, according to Kwan, was that we should not be so concerned when we had these alerts every so often. They were really no big deal at all. I took him for his word on this, but I still got somewhat nervous when the sirens went off on the Post.

On the 25th of January 1972, I officially became a SP/4 in the U.S. Army. This happened a week before my departure for Japan, and I was required to take a drug test before I left the country. This, by the way, was one of the most degrading things I have ever had to do in my life. Have you ever tried to urinate into a bottle while two other guys stand there and watch to see if you are putting some foreign substance in the bottle instead of pee? The whole thing was disgusting but it was required. I did manage to pass the test though, and everything was a go for my leave to Japan. I couldn't wait to get out of Korea for a little while, even if I wasn't going back to the United States. At that point in time, just about anywhere was better than where I was in Korea. You know the old adage: "It was a nice place to visit, but I wouldn't want to live there." That definitely applied to Korea.

On the 31st of January, my official leave arrived and I was off to Japan military-style. I chose to fly military-style because although we could fly commercially, flying military-style was free on a space-available basis. There were daily flights from Korea to Japan and back and you could arrange for them in advance. But traveling this way was slightly different than just getting on a plane to go somewhere for vacation. Three of us left Camp Red Cloud by bus at around 2:00 in the afternoon, arriving first at Osan Air Force Base at around 6:00 in the evening. We had to wait for about three hours for a flight to Japan on a Southern Airways military flight. The flight to Japan took nearly six hours, with a stopover at Kunsan Air Force Base to pick up more guys going on leave and so forth. We arrived at Yakota Air Force Base near Tokyo, Japan at around 11:45 p.m.

It took another two hours to arrange transportation from the airport to the Transient quarters, which were also free. The military provided barracks for soldiers traveling between duty stations and for those on leave. It wasn't like staying in a hotel, but it did come with maid service. They had a Mess Hall, and there were usually restaurants you could go to for your meals if you were willing to pay for them. This made for a cheap way to see the world for those of us on a limited budget.

The three of us traveling together slept in until around 11:30 a.m. on the 1st of February. The accommodations were far superior to our barracks in Korea. It was almost like staying at a Holiday Inn—but not quite. I could tell that the Air Force guys knew how to live in a foreign country. The thought occurred to me more than once during this 10-day leave as to why I hadn't enlisted in the Air Force instead of waiting to be drafted by the Army. From what I saw, these Air Force guys had it made in the shade when it came to serving in the military. The conditions for living and working were far superior to anything the Army offered. I am not saying that these guys were a bunch of pampered wimps, but they sure had things better than we did in Korea. There were even American women running around on the base. We were definitely in culture shock.

Our first stop in Japan was the PX, which is where I purchased a 35-millimeter camera and plenty of film for our excursion. I spent $54 on all of this stuff, which was a lot of money back in those days but it was a lot cheaper than trying to buy this stuff in the States. I got the camera for about half the price that it would have cost me back at home. After having lunch, the three of us took off for Tokyo. One of the guys had been to Japan before so the other guy and I let him lead the way as to where to go. We boarded a train, and after a 45-minute ride we arrived at Tokyo Central Station. From there we took a subway train down to the Ginza, which is a major shopping district with high-end stores in the heart of downtown Tokyo.

We walked by the Imperial Palace, and we spent a little time looking around at everything. It was kind of overcast and rainy that first day so picture-taking was not really on the agenda. While on this walk we encountered a couple of other G.I.'s, and after getting a few directions from them we made our way to the USO office. We also picked up some information about guided tours that were available during our stay in Japan. Most of the guides, by the way, turned out to be female, and most of them were cute and friendly. They were all Japanese, of course, but a guy couldn't ask for everything. Expecting Ann Margaret to show up to take us on a guided tour of Tokyo was a little unrealistic.

After messing around in Tokyo for a few hours, we then returned to Yakota Air Force Base and went out for pizza and beers. The other two guys turned in early to get some rest. They had arranged for a tour the following day. I went back over to the airport to wait for another buddy of mine to come in by plane. We were going to bum around together for a few days. "Thumper" arrived at around 11:00 p.m. from Korea. We got back to the Transient quarters and eventually arranged to get a room together.

I must digress for a few moments now. As I have mentioned before, I have purposely left people's real names out of this book. When the other guys that I was in the Service with found out that I intended to someday write a book about my time in the Army, they all made me swear to a quasi blood oath that I wouldn't divulge any names to protect the innocent, so to speak. Some of our escapades in Korea were less-than-upstanding in nature. So I have taken the liberty of using their nicknames instead. We all had a nickname given to us by the other guys. Mine was "Lima Foxtrot," which was Army lingo for "Little Fucker." Our nicknames were given to us based on our most outstanding physical or mental attributes. Since I was the shortest guy no matter where I seemed to go, I was the Little Fucker.

You can just imagine how Thumper got his nickname. First of all, he was a very big guy at around 6'3" or so. He also had the biggest feet that I have ever seen other than on basketball players. Everybody must have agreed and designated him as the "Thumper." He and I became good friends right away after his arrival in Korea a couple of months or so after I arrived in the country. He was a professional photographer in civilian life. He and I were kind of thrown together working on assignments for *The Gauntlet* newspaper. I would write the stories and he would do the photography work. The Army, in all of its wisdom, made Thumper a Chaplain's Assistant. In other words, he was the Chaplain's official driver. Thumper also did clerical work and ran errands as needed. He was kind of like a grown-up altar boy.

They gave him a position, but Thumper's main job was photography. Anytime anything was happening of any importance that needed pictures taken, Thumper was the go-to guy. He and I did a lot of running around in Korea taking pictures and writing news stories for *The Gauntlet*. Apparently, having a professional photographer and a professional writer within the Brigade was very rare, and the Army made use of our talents on a regular basis.

In any case, we started bumming around together and had a great time while we were in Korea. We were both single and without girlfriends at home, so we kind of shared the same views on things. We were quite a sight together as one tall guy and one short guy walking down the street. It made for some interesting situations when we were out on the town searching for female companionship.

The following day after his arrival in Japan, Thumper and I started out at around 7:00 a.m. After a small breakfast we headed for Tokyo for the day. We took a train and then the subway, and we ended up in the Ginza district at around 9:45 a.m. We went over to the USO and arranged for a tour of the city. Our guide for the day was a cute little girl about 18 years old named Aiko. After our introductions, we sat down with her and explained that we wanted to see some of the highlights of the city. We left it up to her to decide where we would go and what we would see that day. She took us first to the Imperial Palace. We then traveled to the Tokyo Tower and took a tour of that structure. By that time we were pretty hungry. Food was the next order of business. For that we went to a place called Shinjuku, where we ate tempura and tried our hand at using chopsticks. Our guide got quite a chuckle out of that. We got somewhat proficient at it, but I am sure she thought we were nuts.

After lunch we traveled to the Meiji Shrine. Aiko explained that it was built in commemoration of the Emperor Meiji, who was the grandfather of the present emperor of Japan. According to our guide, Emperor Meiji was one of the most loved emperors in the history of Japan. Aiko guided us through the ritual of cleansing ourselves before entering the shrine. She showed us how to pray. We also walked through several beautiful gardens at the shrine. We made a wish for future success and prosperity while we were there.

Throughout the day, Thumper and I spent our time kidding around with Aiko to see her reaction to things. She must have thought that we were just a couple of crazy Americans. Aiko was a very bright and serious young lady. She went to great lengths to explain everything to us. She was very well-spoken—she actually probably spoke English better than we did. We were always joking with her throughout our travels. I am not sure that she fully understood our sense of humor. For example, while walking down a sidewalk in the Ginza, she was slightly ahead of us. She inadvertently walked under a ladder that was propped up against a building where workers were cleaning the windows. We started laughing hysterically at this point. She gave us a curious look, and we had to explain to her that it was considered bad luck in our country to walk under ladders. Once she fully understood the significance of what she had casually done, we all got a big laugh out of it. Being somewhat shy, she started blushing a little since she was laughing out loud in public. She did say that she would never walk under a ladder again. We finished our day in Tokyo with a McDonald's hamburger, of all things. It was very strange though. Here we were 10,000 miles from home, and we were eating a burger and fries under the Golden Arches.

It snowed the following day, so Thumper and I decided to stick around on the base and hit the PX again. I bought some gifts for my parents' birthdays and picked up some accessories for my newly purchased camera. Thumper helped with this project since he was my resident expert on photography. For the most part, we just relaxed and messed around all day. We also discussed our game plan for the following day and then turned in later that night.

The next day began with us sleeping in. We slept so long that we missed breakfast altogether. We headed for the Ginza after lunch on the base. We reached the Ginza at around 3:00 p.m. We had decided the night before that we would spend this day exploring the city on our own. First we spent about two hours shopping in the various shops and stores in the Ginza. We walked through the Matsuya store, which is comparable to a Marshall Fields store in the States. I managed to purchase a very nice ski sweater while we were there. It was a little difficult since most of the employees spoke virtually no English. Trying to get a clerk to give me an opinion on how the sweater looked on me was an adventure. All I received was a lot of curious looks and giggles from the very shy girls working there. I finally decided that they probably thought the sweater looked OK on me, but I wasn't for sure on that.

After our shopping excursion we went back to the USO and signed up for a tour of the nightlife in Tokyo. We took a cab to the exclusive Dai Ichi Hotel, where we were then picked up by the tour bus. Our first stop on the tour was at a very fancy Kobe Beef restaurant where we had a very tasty fried beef dinner with noodles and veggies. We also had a couple of cups of Sake to wash down the food. We were feeling real warm and happy by the time we finished dinner. Our next stop was the famous Nichigichi Music Hall, where we enjoyed a very high-class burlesque show.

We traveled to the Cordon Bleu after the show. This was an exclusive nightclub where we had some more Sake and enjoyed another floor show with topless dancers. Thumper and I, being true red-blooded American boys, enjoyed the heck out of this show. The girls were not exactly well-endowed on top, but they all had great legs and very few clothes on during their performances. According to our guide, this club was very exclusive and was normally only frequented by the very rich and influential people in Japan.

We topped our evening on the town with a stop at a real-life Geisha House. We ate snacks and drank a lot more Sake while the geisha girls entertained us with music and so forth. Thumper, being a very large guy, got a lot of attention because he had a hell of a time crossing his legs to sit down. We took a lot of pictures while we were there, and Thumper and I, feeling no pain from all of the Sake, were quite jovial throughout our time there. We got back to the base at around 1:00 a.m. We were totally drunk at this point and had no trouble falling asleep.

The next day started at around 9:30 a.m. with Thumper and I both suffering with severe hangovers from the previous night. The Winter Olympics were going on in Sapporo, Japan. We decided to stay on the base, hit the PX again, and watch the 70-meter ski jump event on TV. We had considered going to the Olympics while we were in Japan, but a lack of funds and time caused us to be like everyone else—television-watchers. We simply watched the events on TV in between our excursions. Besides, everywhere we went there were TV's televising the Olympics anyway.

Monday, February 7th was another lousy day for weather in Japan. Thumper and I basically messed around on the base again. Since it was another lost day, we went to the PX and picked up a few more things to take back to Korea. Some of the guys in the unit had asked us to pick up some things for them while we were in Japan. Thumper bought a couple of things for his Korean girlfriend at the time. We then called the USO and made arrangements for two guides for Tuesday. We had decided that it would be more fun if we each had a guide for the day. We could go on a quasi double-date of sorts. We went to the Italian Hideaway Restaurant on the base Monday night. We had a full-course Italian meal, which included wine since we were fairly recovered from our hangovers from the previous outing.

We awoke early on that Tuesday and headed for Tokyo during the morning rush hour. That was an adventure in itself. After boarding the train, the car we were riding in quickly filled up with commuters going to work in the city. In fact, it got so full of people that we were packed in this car like sardines in a can. Fortunately, everyone had apparently taken a bath that morning. It seemed like every stop we made the whole car unloaded and then filled back up with people again. Thumper and I were jostled around and were forced at one point right up against the doors. And as you might have guessed, when the train stopped we were shoved out on the platform. It took all of our efforts to get back on the train before it left the station. So much for politeness and looking out for tourists.

We met our two female guides at 10:00 a.m. at the USO downtown. After talking with them, we found out that this was their first day on the job. They were naturally shy and somewhat unsure of themselves. Thumper and I tried to make them feel at ease by joking around with them a little. We took them out for coffee and planned our day's activities. Our first stop was the Asakaya Temple. Since it was a nice sunny day we took loads of pictures. By the time we finished visiting that place it was time for lunch. We rode a short distance on the subway to get closer to our next destination.

We told the girls that we wanted to go to a traditional Japanese restaurant and eat a lunch that a normal Japanese person would eat instead of going to some Americanized place. They thought about this for a few moments and then proceeded to take us to a place right on the street in downtown Tokyo. We got a few strange looks from some of the other customers, but we were not swayed from our intentions. We had the girls order all of the food since Thumper and I had no idea what to order. We ended up getting what the Japanese call "sandwiches and Cokes" all around. The Japanese idea of a sandwich is slightly different than you might imagine. Our meal consisted of a plate of several little rice cakes with raw fish on top of them. It was our understanding from our guides that we were eating octopus, squid, tuna, eel, and shrimp. Our only mistake was that each time we picked up one of these little sandwiches we would ask what exactly we were eating. Most of it was fairly tolerable. I think I gagged a couple of times on the octopus, squid, and eel, but for the most part it was very enjoyable. Good conversation with the girls and a lot of Coke did the trick.

We visited the Tokyo Tower for the second time, and we actually saw quite a bit more than we did the first time. Next we traveled to the Shinjuku Imperial Garden. We must have stayed there for a couple of hours or more taking pictures and so forth. We were having so much fun that we completely lost track of time. The next thing we knew, it was about 4:25 p.m. and we were nowhere near the entrance to the park. The problem was that the Garden closed to the public at 4:30 p.m. So as you might have guessed, we got locked inside. Our guides were completely flustered by this turn of events. However, Thumper and I used our good old American ingenuity to get us out of this predicament.

We found a secluded part of the Garden and climbed over the stone wall back onto the street. I scaled the wall first so I was forced to catch the girls on the other side of the wall as they climbed over it. I was very cavalier, and I received them both with open arms and a helping hand or two. After all, I was brought up to be nothing but a gentleman in these kinds of situations. These were upstanding college girls working for their educations! After that harrowing experience, Thumper and I decided that we had no other alternative but to buy the girls something to eat. We splurged and took them to McDonald's for dinner. We returned the girls to the USO and then went back to the base for our last evening in Japan. All and all, we had a grand time.

The following day was spent traveling back to Korea with us arriving back at good old Camp Red Cloud just before curfew. I ended up working the last two days of that week and tried to catch up on the paperwork that I had left 10 days earlier. My desk was piled with paper, and it took both days to catch up on everything. I also caught up with what was going on in the Battery from my new roommate, "Taksan Man." Apparently, I hadn't missed much during my 10 days in Japan. My desk at work said otherwise, but who was complaining? Everybody had a job to do, and you always pay the price for going on vacation.

CHAPTER EIGHTEEN:

Orderly Room Honcho, Promotion, and the Annual General Inspection

I became the official Orderly Room honcho about three weeks after my return from Japan. I received this honor by default since I was now the only one left in the office. To my great surprise, I learned that there were no immediate plans to bring in any more clerks. Either I had become so good at my job that the powers-that-be decided I didn't need any help, or there weren't any new guys coming into the country who could type. I wasn't sure which was correct. In any case, I was now doing the work of three guys. It created a pile of paperwork that seemed to never go away. It would stay that way until I was within 60 days of leaving Korea myself. In a way it was a good situation. I no longer had any lazy afternoons waiting for the phone to ring. The bad part was that I now barely had time to answer the phone period!

I spent the first couple of weeks working well past the 5:00 p.m. hour catching up on an increasing pile of paperwork. I even worked a few Saturday mornings on my own to keep things on an even keel. Amazingly, by the 1st of March I had things running pretty smoothly and had settled into my new role. I felt a lot like Radar on the TV show "Mash" sometimes. There were days that were really crazy and full of mass confusion, which was what was often depicted on that TV series.

It was around this same time that the current Battery Commander and the First Sergeant rotated out of the Battery, and I had two new bosses to deal with. Of course they both had their own ideas about how things should be run in the organizational structure of the Battery. There were a few testy moments at the beginning of their tours at HQ Battery. However, after a few weeks I had them both convinced that I really knew what I was doing, and they pretty much left the administration of the office to me. I obviously had the advantage of knowing everyone in the Battery, I knew where everything was, and I knew how to get things done to cut through all of the red tape that occurred in the Army's scheme of things.

In other words, I knew all of the tricks to cut corners and get around the chain of command. To really get things done you never went to the officer in charge of a certain department. You always called his clerk. The clerks were the guys actually running the various departments. The officers were there simply to sign the paperwork and oversee the administration. They very rarely got directly involved in the work. Once in a while you had to deal directly with an officer, but if you said all the right things and showed the proper respect you could talk them into things too. One of my biggest problems when I was talking to these various departments was that I was only a SP/4 in rank. Invariably, I would call a department and would end up talking to a Staff Sergeant or another First Sergeant. Most of these guys were "lifers" (career Army types), and they for the most part had little regard for draftees like myself or lower-ranked clerks.

Shortly after the new Battery Commander's and the new First Sergeant's arrivals on the scene, I explained to them that what would make my job a lot easier since I was the only one left to do the work was if they provided me with a solution to most of these problems. After a short deliberation, they decided to promote me again! One month after being promoted to SP/4 I was promoted to the rank of Acting Sergeant. I of course had the distinct pleasure of typing up my own promotion orders again. From then on whenever I made calls out or answered the phone I was now "Sergeant Poindexter speaking." This gave me a lot of clout when dealing with people. In a lot of cases the Officers and Sergeants I talked to thought they were talking to the actual Battery First Sergeant. I never discouraged them from thinking anything different. I very rarely gave them the idea that they were talking to a lowly clerk.

This also worked to the advantage of the Battery Commander and the First Sergeant. With the upcoming annual General Inspection on the horizon, they had to spend a lot of time out of the office checking things out in the various areas and departments throughout the Battery. Quite often I was left on my own to essentially run the administration of the Battery. I technically couldn't sign all of the paperwork but I did everything else. My job had suddenly taken on a whole new perspective. It was actually starting to get interesting! I took on many new roles and really got into my work. My time in Korea started flying by, and the weeks and months rolled by in a much less tedious manner.

I took a lot of ribbing from my roommate and other friends in regard to my promotion to Sergeant. Every chance they had they all started calling me "Sarge." No matter what the conversation was they would always say, "What do you think, Sarge?" They made every effort to be as obnoxious as they could in this regard. My only defense against all of this hazing was to threaten them with bodily harm. Since I was probably the smallest guy in the Battery they never took me very seriously on these threats. Once they knew they were irritating me they would go to great lengths to make fun of the whole situation. I never really got mad about all of this, but they really got carried away with the ribbing.

Anyway, by the middle of March I was settling into my new role as the Orderly Room honcho of HQ Battery, 2nd, 71st, ADA. There were a couple of times in particular when my elevated rank of Sergeant really came into play. First of all, HQ Battery had several detachments in off-Post locations around Uijongbu. Each detachment had its own First Sergeant and office clerk. However, all of the paperwork for the Battery had to come through the Orderly Room for approval from the First Sergeant or the Battery Commander. It was one of my many tasks to weed through all of this paper and review it, correct it, re-type it, etc., before running it through the bosses for approval.

One of these detachments was the Direct Support Platoon (DSP). It consisted of a motor pool and a maintenance facility for all of the vehicles connected with our operation as a HAWK Missile Battalion. I had a lot of hassles when dealing with this group's First Sergeant and office clerk during my stint in the Orderly Room. First of all, they always had a hard time getting things over to me on a timely basis. Almost every piece of paperwork they sent over needed re-typing or correcting before I could submit it for approval from the bosses. After a while it was getting ridiculous. I had several heated discussions with the clerk who was sending this stuff over to me, and I was getting nowhere trying to convince him that it was his responsibility to get this stuff right before he sent it over to the Orderly Room. I tried to explain to him that I had way too many things to do myself and that I didn't have time to keep correcting and re-typing all of his work. I tried to enlist the support of his First Sergeant in this regard. That also failed because he had very little regard for some smart-ass SP/4 clerk trying to tell him or his clerk how things had to be done.

To make a long story short, I was finally forced to go to the Battery Commander and the First Sergeant and explain my situation to them. We discussed things, and they agreed that I was in need of better cooperation from these guys. The DSP First Sergeant was called into HQ and we all sat down for a conference. Of course, by the time this meeting took place I had already received my promotion to Acting Sergeant and I was wearing my nice new shiny stripes on my uniform. It was explained to the DSP First Sergeant that I ,"Sgt. Poindexter," was in charge of all day-to-day administration of the Orderly Room. He was also instructed to cooperate with me and to see to it that his clerk did the same. I know that this "lifer" First Sergeant was not happy and hated my little ass, but I did get better-quality work out of his clerk and much more cooperation after that. Before I left Korea there were several other times when I had to talk with these guys for something, and we sort of reached a mutual understanding so to speak. We weren't friends by any means, but we tolerated each other.

On another occasion I was hard at work on my morning report when I received a call from the Command Sergeant Major over at Battalion. He asked me if a certain individual was a member of the HQ Battery. I replied that he was a member of the unit. The CSM then proceeded to tell me that I had exactly one hour to get this guy in the Orderly Room and have him packed and ready to leave the country on a general discharge. The only problem was that the Battery Commander and the First Sergeant were out for the day doing things for the upcoming General Inspection. After some serious scrambling on my part, I actually got this guy tracked down, packed, and ready to leave the unit in the required time. As for signing the actual paperwork involved, the CSM basically told me to sign this guy out of the unit. This kind of stuff usually required the signature of the Battery Commander for it to be official. The CSM told me not to worry about it and that he would take responsibility if anybody questioned the paperwork.

In spite of his assurance, I was still a little concerned so I came up with an idea on how to handle this and still be completely in the clear on the issue. I went ahead and signed the Captain's name on the document in my best forgery, and then I initialed it with my rank below his name. I have to admit that it was a pretty good forgery. I probably could have let it stand on its own, but I wanted to take the safest course of action.

When the Battery Commander and the First Sergeant returned from their inspection tour, they asked me if anything had happened while they were gone. I casually said, "Oh nothing really. I just got rid of one of your personnel while you were gone, that's all." The Captain said, "How in the hell did you do that without my signature on the paperwork?" I then produced our copy of the documents and showed him his name signed on all of the papers. He gave me a curious look for a moment or two. I wasn't sure whether he was mad or what. After a couple moments of silence he said, "Sgt. Poindexter, next time make the 'L' a little bigger with more of a loop at the bottom." He then walked into his office and nothing further was said about the incident.

From then on I started signing his name for him on a regular basis. He apparently did not have a problem with this because he never said to stop doing it. Once in a while I would do something that I thought I should get his actual signature on, such as on orders and promotions, etc., but for the most part I took care of everything else myself. I probably could have typed and signed my own way out of the unit, but being a loyal and patriotic soldier I never thought of trying that stunt. I did, however, give myself frequent weekend passes to leave the Post. As long as I was back at work on Monday morning nobody gave a shit.

We endured the annual General Inspection around the middle of March 1972. This involved people from the 38th Brigade coming to our unit for an annual audit of our files, paperwork, condition of the Battery, and so forth. They were checking to see that we were following the Army's Standard Operating Procedure on things, and they were also looking to see if we were in "operational readiness." This was a two-day affair, and I had several inspectors in and out of the Orderly Room looking at everything that I was doing then and had done in the past. They asked a million questions and expected quick answers from me. Trust me, I was really scrambling for a couple of days. After all, I hadn't been the Orderly Room honcho for that long at the time. I must have talked the right talk and danced the right dance over those two days though because we came through the inspection with flying colors. My new Battery Commander and First Sergeant were very grateful to say the least. They treated me to another breakfast!

CHAPTER NINETEEN:

An Afternoon With Kwan and His Family

Perhaps the most rewarding and truly memorable experience of my stay in Korea occurred on March 18, 1972. Takson Man, Thumper, and I all had Kwan as our houseboy, and the three of us had become pretty close friends with him over the many months we were together. We kept trying to talk him into taking us out to his home in Uijongbu to meet his family. For many months he resisted the idea thinking that we were just messing around with him. But we really just wanted to see how he lived. After a while he realized that we were actually serious about it. We convinced him that our intentions were nothing but honorable and that we would be willing to supply all of the beer and pop for the party.

Armed with about 30 cans of beer and two six-packs of Coke, the three of us headed out to the Village. We arrived at Kwan's home at around 4:00 in the afternoon. He lived in a gated courtyard in an L-shaped house with several separate rooms that were all maybe 10 feet by 10 feet in size. They had an old-style hand pump for water and an outhouse. The place was pretty upscale by Korean standards. Heating for the rooms was provided by charcoal bricks that were heated up and then were slid under the floor in each room. Each room had linoleum flooring and throw rugs. They didn't have a lot of furniture, and they apparently slept on the floor on mats. Laundry was hanging on ropes stretched across the courtyard. There was what appeared to be an old iron cookstove for preparing meals and heating water for baths.

Kwan ushered us into one of the empty rooms, and we sat down and talked for a while over a couple of beers. After about a half-hour, it was time for Kwan to introduce us to his family. He was really funny about it and made a big production out of the whole thing. He introduced his four children one at a time starting with the oldest one first. His oldest child was a girl about 10 years old. The next one was also a girl about 8 years old, and then there was a boy about 4 years old. Finally, Kwan's sister-in-law came in with his baby girl who was about 1 1/2 years old. None of the kids spoke a word of English and they were all very shy. They were not sure what to make of us G.I.'s. Kwan's sister-in-law was a very attractive woman in her early 30's.

We asked the kids different questions with Kwan interpreting for us. They were all very well-behaved and only spoke when they were asked something. The two older girls talked between themselves in hushed tones. I am sure the two of them had a lot to say about us crazy Americans. The little boy was the most outgoing, and you could see that he was Kwan's favorite. He kept leaning over and whispering in his dad's ear, and you could see that he was very curious about what we were doing at their house. After about 20 minutes or so, the kids were ushered out by the sister-in-law and we were then introduced to Kwan's wife and her other sister. They stayed for a few moments and then scurried off to prepare our dinner.

Kwan's little boy came back in and got to stay with the guys for dinner. The women and the girls ate in another room. We then started into what ended up being a several-course meal. We had bowls of rice; one-half of a chicken each; two different kinds of Kimchi; fried eggs; another mixture of eggs and spinach; a beef eggroll and some other kind of greens mixture; and a couple of other sweet broths, one with rice in it and the other with what appeared to be seaweed. I am not sure what exactly it was, but it had the texture of cellophane. It was all quite tasty and very filling. We washed it all down with several Budweiser's and PBR's. By the end of the afternoon we were all stuffed, tipsy, and happy.

After eating this fabulous dinner, Kwan's kids returned for the rest of our visit. We had a hidden tape recorder with us, and we taped our conversations with Kwan during dinner. His kids sang some Korean songs for us and we continued to interact with them with Kwan serving as the interpreter. All of this was recorded unbeknownst to the kids. And we took loads of pictures of the family as the day went along too.

Somewhere along the line Kwan's little boy discovered that we had the recorder. So after the kids sang all of their songs we played back our recording for everyone. We got a lot of laughs out of this. Like anywhere else in the world, people don't really realize what they say or do until somebody records it and plays it back for them. It was truly hilarious, and Kwan got quite a chuckle out of it. His kids did a lot of embarrassed giggling at hearing their voices in a recorded fashion. Our best communication with the kids actually came through music. We tried to remember our childhood songs that we had all learned in grade school. After we would sing them to the kids, they would sing them back to us in Korean. They knew almost all of them! We also taught them the hand tricks of the "Here's the church and the steeple, open the doors, and see all the people." Thumper even came up with several shadow tricks on the wall to entertain the kids.

The following week we were surprised to find out from Kwan that we were the first Americans to ever be in his house. He had been a houseboy for several years, and apparently we were the first G.I.'s he trusted enough to be allowed to see how he and his family lived. That was very surprising, and we felt honored to have been the first ones. I for one will always remember that afternoon as one of my fondest memories of my time in the Service. It was proof that different cultures can get along if we really work at it.

I think our government does a lot of good things around the world, but I often think that we sometimes are so enamored with our own successes that we seem pushy and arrogant to other people. The fact is that what works over here in the States may not work in other places. We must always take into account that different cultures exist and we must respect their rights and beliefs when dealing with them. People from other countries are just as proud of their history as we are of our history. Their history may not be at the same level of success as ours, but it is still their history just the same. There have been many cultures in the history of the world that have been in existence a lot longer than our culture has. Just because we think we are right doesn't mean that they think we are right. This is something that our leaders should think about.

CHAPTER TWENTY:

Shot-Gunning, The Cab Ride, and Easter in Korea

Over the next three weeks following our visit to Kwan's house for dinner, I started to get really busy as Orderly Room honcho and in my new role as the "Sarge." I was to find out that with my new rank came further duties I had not anticipated. Every so often the Battery Commander or the First Sergeant would send me on an errand that they didn't want to fool with. For example, every vehicle that left the Post had to have a driver and an E/5-type (sergeant-level) NCO riding shotgun. The NCO was required to carry a sidearm at all times. As these situations came along, the Battery Commander would send me over to the Armory to get his 45 pistol to use as my sidearm. I really wasn't proficient at shooting it for real but it looked good.

When you were riding "shotgun" for the guy doing the driving in a combat or semi-combat zone, we were required to carry a weapon along with ammunition in case of an ambush or some other dangerous occurrence. Sometimes we were escorting personnel going out on less-than-honorable discharges or we were moving them to a detention center. The weapon that was typically assigned to me was an M-16 assault rifle, but to prevent having to carry it around with me the Battery Commander would let me use his 45 pistol for these trips. It had a holster and belt and everything.

Some of these errands included taking outgoing officers to Seoul or picking officers up at the airport. Sometimes there was correspondence that had to go to Brigade and it couldn't wait on the mail system. Well, since Thumper always had access to the Chaplain's vehicle and had a driver's license to drive in Korea, he became my official driver. When we went on these errands, Thumper and I took these opportunities to see a little bit of the country as well. We often went off the normal routes to places, and we traveled the country roads through villages where G.I.'s normally did not go during their off-time. Most of these roads were gravel rather than paved highways. They also had Korean Army checkpoints every so often to make sure that we didn't end up in North Korea by accident.

The procedure when you approached one of these checkpoints was to come to a complete stop so that the guard could identify you. Once he determined that you were one of the good guys he would wave you on through the checkpoint. Most of the time this was not a big deal and we went through these checkpoints without a hitch. We were on one of these side trips one day when we managed to make this an exciting event, however. As I mentioned before, my buddy Thumper was one of those laid-back California guys who never seemed to get flustered by anything. His driving style very much reflected how he was in real life. Anyway, on one of our excursions we were approaching one of these checkpoints and Thumper casually rolled up to it. He made one of those rolling stops like you would do at a stop sign out in the country. The guard was a little slow coming out of the guard house to identify us, so Thumper started to take off again. As we passed the guard I heard him say something to us, but we kept going down the road. As I turned around to look at him I saw him starting to level his M-16 at us. Then he realized that we were just a couple of goofy G.I.'s. He gave us a middle-fingered salute and decided that we were not infiltrators. Luckily, he let us go on our merry way.

I yelled at Thumper saying, "What are you trying to do? Get us killed?" I told him that at the next checkpoint we came to we had better stop and wait for the guard to wave us through. Thumper was not worried about any of this, so I worried for both of us. He told me that he always did it that way and nothing ever happened. I asked for my own peace of mind that he make complete stops from then on. He complied with my wishes, but I don't think he ever quite figured out what I was all wound up about. I may have overreacted a little on this but being a non-combatant clerk and not a Green Beret, I preferred to take the least line of resistance in these types of situations. Avoiding tense situations always seemed like the prudent course of action. Besides, I thought of the amount of paperwork that I would have to type up explaining how Thumper and I managed to get 20 rounds of ammunition embedded in the Battery Commander's Jeep!

A group of us went down to Seoul to a place called E-Tae-Won a few days before the Easter holiday. This was about a 20-mile ride from Uijongbu. Our mode of transportation was a cab. This was normally not a big deal as long as you had enough Korean money with you and it wasn't too close to curfew. This usually was never a big problem for us level-headed, red-blooded, all-American G.I.'s. We were often very resourceful in our efforts to comply with this policy.

E-Tae-Won was the nightclub district near the Yong-Song compound in Seoul. It was a real jumping place most every night. Some of the most beautiful girls in Korea were all at this one location, and they were a definite upgrade from the local gals in Uijongbu. Every club that we went to had a live band and a dance floor. We were really having a blast on this particular evening. Great music, beautiful women, and plenty of beer bolstered our bravery against the "elements." The "elements" was a funny word we had for having to fight off the many advances by girls or their Mamasans to get you to take them home for less-than-honorable activities. There were also loads of street vendors everywhere you went trying to sell you a wide variety of items and food.

After visiting a few of the clubs, we were brave enough for just about any mission we were required to handle. In other words, we were all drunk as skunks and feeling very little pain. We were all having such a great time that we lost complete track of it. Before we knew it, curfew was less than an hour away and we were 20 miles from Uijongbu! Little did we realize that our evening's adventure was just beginning, however. Our first problem was to find a cab that would take us all the way to Uijongbu. The second problem was that we were all out of money to pay for it.

Undaunted, we started our search for a cab. After all, the objective was to get back close enough to the Post that we could walk through the gate before curfew went into effect. After a few minutes we secured a cab, and the cabbie said that he could get us about halfway to where we wanted to go. We could then transfer to his cousin's cab and finish the trip. You see, Koreans had to be off the streets by midnight just like we did. We solved the problem of our lack of funding by assuring the first cabbie that we would pay his cousin for the trip once we arrived near the Post. We insisted that we would not pay until we had arrived at our destination. This was not an unusual situation. When you went out into the Ville no matter what you did or bought, there was always a negotiation that took place before arriving at the final price. There was no set price for anything. It was more whatever the market could bear. Sometimes it worked out OK for you, and other times you were screwed.

The first cabbie agreed to our demands. We sealed the deal by offering him several American cigarettes and shooting the breeze with him along the way. We successfully made the transfer to the other cab by basically using the same method. The fact that we were short of funds did not deter us from driving a hard bargain on the price of the trip. Well, after arriving near the Post stage two of our plan was initiated. We had decided that we would use the "I'll get it" routine once we arrived at our destination. Once we were within a couple hundred yards of the Post, we told the cabbie that this was far enough and he pulled over to the curb. We got out of the cab one at a time and began our little rouse. The first guy announced "I'll get it." The second guy said, "No, I'll get it," and then by that time I was out of the cab and I said "No, no, I'll get it." At this point we all took off running in different directions down the street and into the alleys. Needless to say, the cabbie was pissed and he started calling us every name in the Korean dictionary! He stood there shaking his fists at us while we were running at breakneck speed to find a place to hide out in.

After about five minutes, the cabbie gave up on his pursuit of getting his money. There was only about 10 minutes of street time left before curfew. So he took off in his cab and we reconvened at a preselected location. We then casually walked through the gate at Camp Red Cloud at precisely 11:59 p.m. We had arrived right at the last minute before curfew. The guards at the gate thought nothing of all of this since it was an every night occurrence for G.I.'s to show up just under the wire for curfew. We all had a great laugh about this while we trudged back to the barracks. We even bragged about how slick we all were in stiffing the cabbies. We justified this behavior by all agreeing that at some point during our stay in Korea we had all been screwed at one time or another by some Korean vendor or businesswoman. Paybacks were hell!

I served my penance a couple of days later with the arrival of Easter Sunday. I attended church services, and I prayed for forgiveness of my dastardly deeds and misbehavior over the weekend. Besides, I was sure that the guy upstairs was a forgiving God and would understand that I was basically a good soul in the long run. I really had no choice. It was like the old saying, "When in Rome, do as the Romans do." I was simply following the normal code of conduct that most Koreans expect from crazy Americans.

I can recall one evening when a bunch of us were returning to the Post from the Ville and were watching a very large G.I. running for his life up the street. He was closely followed by a tiny Korean businesswoman who had a meat cleaver in her hand and was screaming at the top of her lungs. He had obviously stiffed her for her services or had really made her mad about something.

CHAPTER TWENTY-ONE:

One-Golf, Softball, Bike Rides, and Flu Shots

With the Easter holiday behind us, the troops at Camp Red Cloud began to plan our activities for the upcoming spring and summer months. These included the formation of our Battery and Battalion golf and softball teams. I, being an involved sports fanatic in those days, decided to participate in both activities. I also determined that I was much better at these sports than basketball. My lack of height had doomed me from the beginning to play on the basketball team. I tried very hard to use my shifty moves and overall quickness to overcome the obvious one big shortcoming that I had. This experiment, for the most part, had failed miserably. I played very little during our games, but at least I participated. Besides, keeping busy was a major problem with life in the Army. Boredom was as big an adversary as the North Koreans.

I was determined to have a bigger impact on the golf and softball teams. These were two sports that I was actually pretty good at. I golfed during my high school days, and I had played on a church league softball team for a number of years prior to my time in the Service. I felt reasonably sure that I could hold my own against the jocks in the Battery and the Battalion. Making the Battalion golf team was quite easy, as it turned out. There were only a few guys who played golf in the first place. Competition for spots on the team was not that intense. Most of the Neanderthals in the Battalion were too busy going to the Ville to chase women and raise hell with the natives. There was a small core of us who played golf on a regular basis, so we as a group decided that we would form the Battalion golf team.

After some fast-talking with the Command Sergeant Major, we convinced him that it would really be an honor to represent our Battalion in a Brigade golf tournament. We had made some contacts with friends in other Battalions throughout the Brigade and we had enough interest to have a golf tournament down in Pusan, Korea. We even convinced the Command Sergeant Major to finance team windbreakers for all of us to wear during the tournament. We cut a deal with one of the local merchants down in the Ville to produce these windbreakers for a nominal cost. They turned out quite nice, and we were the only team with matching jackets when we went to the tournament. As I will relate to you next, having these windbreakers was a stroke of genius on our part. Not only were we the coolest-looking team at the tournament, but the day of the tournament ended up being one of the worst days for golf in recorded history!

Springtime in Korea like in many other countries, is a volatile time of year for weather conditions. Some days were just beautiful, and on other days the weather was for shit. Well, as our luck would have it, the couple of weeks leading up to the big tournament had given us great weather conditions. We were able to get in several rounds of golf and we were honing our skills as a team. We had great aspirations of winning the tournament and taking home trophies from our experience. We were extremely confident that we had one of the best assembled teams in the tournament.

We were given time off from our duties for three days to make the trip to Pusan, play in the tournament, and return the following day. The Command Sergeant Major even came up with a regular four-door sedan for us to travel in rather than a couple of Jeeps. The weather was great the day we drove down to Pusan, and we were able to see the sights and sounds around the Brigade headquarters as we traveled in comfort. We had a nice evening down in Pusan the night before the tournament. We went to several nightclubs and had a luxurious dinner to prime ourselves for the next day's activities.

The next morning we awoke to the sound of rain pounding on the windows of our temporary housing. We were all slightly hungover from the night before, so the fact that the wind was blowing about 30 to 40 miles per hour with a driving rain didn't sink in right away. We just thought that it was a passing storm and our golf tournament would go off without a hitch.

After getting to the golf course and practicing on the putting green while we waited for the other teams to arrive, we noticed that not only was it really cold and windy, but the rain was not going away. We found out from the manager of the golf course that there was a typhoon developing off the coast of Korea and the weather forecast was for really bad conditions as the day went on. But the course was in pretty good shape, and since all of the teams were there to play in the tournament he agreed to let us go ahead with it. Everything had been arranged and paid for well in advance. We even had cute little Korean girls to serve as our caddies and guides.

By the end of the first few holes, we discovered that golfing in a typhoon was not going to be easy. After several slices and grass-burners into the teeth of a now 40- to 50-mile-per-hour wind, we all realized that our hopes for golf glory were going by the wayside very quickly. Even our caddies were enjoying watching us make fools of ourselves in spite of the horrible weather conditions. They were all huddled together at each tee and they had the audacity to giggle and talk among themselves between each of our feeble attempts to hit good golf shots. At least they were having a good time because none of us were! By the time we finished the round of golf, our team was dead last in the tournament. We all agreed that we had played the worst golf of our entire lives.

The trip back to Camp Red Cloud was very somber. We spent the whole time making excuses for our poor performance on the golf course. We, of course, blamed the weather for our lousy scores. My own personal score was well on the high side of 100 for 18 holes. My well-honed 15 handicap was blown right out to sea along with the typhoon. We did agree though that we had had a great time—except for when we were playing golf. Besides, we had gotten out of work for three days at the Army's expense. We were also grateful that we had been so prudent to have gotten the windbreakers made for our team. They had come in handy the day we played in the tournament. We may have finished dead last, but we were the only warm and somewhat dry team at the end of the day. It wasn't much consolation for our poor performance but things could always be worse. Staying in Korea for a while affected your thought processes. After enough consideration on things you could just about rationalize and justify anything if you put your mind to it. We did that a lot during our stay in Korea.

After our rousing success at the golf tournament, we decided that perhaps we would have better results in the fast-pitch softball arena. After all, many of the guys in the Battery had actually played organized baseball as kids, and several of us had played on a church league and on intramural softball teams during our high school days. We were convinced that our chances of success were quite good. Each of the line Batteries in the Battalion formed softball teams, and we set up a season playing each of the teams several times during the spring and summer.

After just a few practices, we at Headquarters Battery realized that we had the makings of a really good team. I tried out at second base and got the position. Back in those days, I was pretty quick on my feet and could cover a lot of ground. I figured that I was a natural for the position. Besides, my arm strength suited itself to shorter throws of the infield variety. I was also made the lead-off man in the lineup. My shortness provided me with the smallest strike zone on the team, and while I wasn't a power hitter by any stretch of the imagination I was pretty good at getting on base with high choppers on the infield or line drives in the gaps. I was also a pretty accomplished bunter. My specialty, however, was getting walked or getting hit by the pitch. In fact, as it turned out I did not get an official at-bat until my eighth attempt. I was walked five times and hit twice before I actually made good contact with the ball. The main thing was that I got on a base and came around to score all seven times at the plate.

After a few games, I was getting very comfortable at second base and leading off in the lineup. Then as luck would have it, during the first week in May we were warming up for a game and getting some infield practice when disaster struck. I was going after a spinning line drive heading for right-field when the ball glanced off my throwing hand and glove, dislocating my right middle finger. The ball hit directly on the end of my finger and turned my nice straight finger into a crooked one in three different directions. Most of the guys thought all of this was pretty funny. I failed to see the humor in it at the time.

My rising success playing softball came to a crashing halt for the next two months. I was taken to the hospital by the medics. The doc looked at my finger and told me that there were two options on how to straighten it back out. He could give me a pain-killing shot first and then jerk my finger back into the right position, or he could just jerk my finger back to straight again and then give me painkillers. In either case it was going to hurt like hell. Being a tough little guy, I opted for the latter choice. I figured that if it was going to hurt no matter which way he did it, why go through the stress of getting a shot too?

I couldn't play again until early July, and I never really hit that well after returning to the team because I had a little trouble gripping the bat and I had limited strength in my finger. I did go to all the games and cheered on the team, but my replacement at second base was more of a liability than an asset, in my opinion. I always felt that I could have helped the team better than my replacement did as the season played out.

The injury also had an effect on my duties in the Orderly Room. Typing was one of my main jobs, so as you might imagine, learning to type with a splint on one of your fingers became problematic at times. I ended up employing the Biblical method of typing for a couple of months—"Seek and Ye Shall Find." I took a lot of kidding and abuse from my buddies during this time. I have to admit, I looked pretty stupid with this very large metal splint on my right middle finger. It did work well for one thing though. When I had heard enough of the verbal abuse I frequently gave them all the proverbial one-fingered salute!

As I have mentioned, getting shots for various reasons has never been one of my favorite things to do. This subject reminds me of one of the funniest things that happened during my tour in Korea. It involved one of my three First Sergeants and the medics. I really don't remember what time of year it was, but at some point it became time for flu shots to be administered to all of the troops. Now in the Army, you really didn't get a choice as to whether you wanted to get one or not. Everybody had to get one. In spite of this mandatory requirement, everybody tried to figure out ways to get out of it.

Sensing that this kind of activity was going on, our First Sergeant came up with a great way to make sure that everyone got their shots. He announced at formation one morning that the only way we would receive our monthly pay at the end of the month was if we went through the shot line first before we went through the pay line. He also announced that since he was requiring this from all of us that he being the very brave and gung-ho First Sergeant that he was, he would be the first guy in line to get the shot.

Now this would have been a brilliant plan except for one little item. During the week leading up to payday, one of the medics happened to come by the Orderly Room one day for something. Unfortunately for him, our very gung-ho First Sergeant happened to be in the office that day and he was on one of his kicks about good grooming and so forth. The medic involved, I have to admit, was a bit shaggy- looking. It had been a while since he had had a haircut and he had a pretty good- looking five o'clock shadow going. As you might imagine, the First Sergeant took it upon himself to totally give this guy the Riot Act and threaten him with disciplinary action. He further instructed this guy to go get a haircut immediately, to shave properly, and to then report back to him looking more like a soldier was supposed to look. As you might have guessed, this did not sit well with the medic. This event in fact started the famous "Flu Shot War" between the medics and the First Sergeant of Headquarters Battery.

Finally, payday arrived. During the few days leading up to the big day, the rumor got around the whole Battery that the medics had big plans for the First Sergeant in the flu shot line. We all waited in anxious anticipation to see what was going to happen. As expected, the First Sergeant lined us all up to receive our flu shots before we could get paid. He, of course, was first in line to get the shot. There were two medics administering the shots, and they were armed with their trusty air-powered shotguns. You had to walk between them and one or the other of them would give you the shot. They did this on purpose to keep you from tensing up while they gave you the shot. Since you didn't know which one it was coming from, you had to relax when you walked between them. By relaxing your muscles before you got the shot, it didn't hurt as much and you saved yourself from other possible trauma such as slicing your arm wide open. This was one time when I was glad to not be a muscle-bound hulk. Anyway, the First

Sergeant walked through the two medics first, and instead of receiving one shot in one arm he got nailed by both of them with one shot in each arm. It happened so fast that he didn't even realize it. He then proceeded to watch over the rest of us while we received our shots.

Now if you receive flu shots on a regular basis, you know that these shots can make your arm sore for a couple of days and that you can have a reaction and actually get the flu in some cases. Well, as expected, everybody's arms were sore for a couple of days, but by the middle of the week my arm was getting back to normal and I had no apparent flu symptoms. The First Sergeant, however, had a different result. I was typing away as usual at around 10:00 a.m., and the First Sergeant was at his desk going over some paperwork. I noticed earlier that morning that he had been flexing his arms quite frequently, but I really didn't give it much thought until he asked me how I was feeling from the flu shot we had all received. I told him that I was doing OK now but that I had been sore for a couple of days. He told me that he was really sore in both arms, and in fact he couldn't lift either arm above his chest. He even admitted that he had to have his houseboy assist him with putting on his uniform every morning.

It took all of my willpower to keep from busting out laughing. I had to bite my tongue several times to not give away the secret that all the rest of us knew. Like a loyal Battery Clerk should do, I consoled the First Sergeant on his plight and recommended that he possibly buy some Ben Gay at the PX to help with his muscle soreness. I even suggested in very empathetic and sympathetic tones that he should possibly make a visit to the hospital and see the doc or one of the medics because of his problem. I knew that this would be his last option being the gung-ho guy that he was, but I suggested the idea anyway.

My act must have worked because he never caught on to what had happened. Being a born pot-stirrer from way back, at the first opportunity I informed every other clerk in the Battery what had gone on between me and the First Sergeant. In no time at all everyone in the Battery except for the First Sergeant knew the whole story. We all had a lot of laughs over this for several months every time the subject came up in conversation. With just a little bit of embellishment, the tale of the great Flu Shot War got funnier and funnier as time went on. It often brought tears to our eyes from laughter.

During the spring and summer months, besides playing golf, softball, and chasing little Korean girls in the Ville, we often came up with other diversions to break up the monotony of military life. We went to movies both on and off the Post, we went shopping in Seoul, we went on picnics out in the country with our current steady girlfriends, and we also took lengthy bike rides. My friend Thumper found out on one of his escapades in the Ville that you could actually rent bicycles for the day for a small fee of a few hundred Won. Now these bicycles were not brand-new, top-of-the-line bikes. They were 1950s vintage bikes with the big balloon tires that some kind soul, probably from America, had donated to the Korean government following the Korean Conflict.

One beautiful Saturday morning, Thumper came over to my cube in the barracks and suggested that we go down to the Ville and rent a couple of these bikes for a ride in the country. Having nothing else planned in my busy schedule, I agreed to his proposition. Since both of us were a little short on cash to go night-clubbing for the afternoon and evening I thought it was a great idea. We walked down to the Ville, rented the bikes, and headed for the countryside. The ride was very challenging in some spots. There were many hills and a lot of gravel roads. Since we really had no plan as to where to go, we ended up going through small villages that we would never have ordinarily seen. In fact, after a short while I became convinced that we were hopelessly lost and probably in North Korea. Thumper kept assuring me that we were not lost and we were instead on the way to one of our line Batteries near the DMZ. We got many funny looks from the villagers as we passed through their little towns. I am sure that they were not used to seeing two G.I.'s, one very tall and one very short, riding old bikes in cut-off shorts and T-shirts.

After a lengthy ride, we finally arrived at "A" Battery near the DMZ. We saw some friends we knew and they invited us to stay for lunch in their Mess Hall. After a couple of hours it was time to head back to good old Camp Red Cloud. The trip up had taken nearly three hours of hard riding, and I was not looking forward to the ride back in spite of Thumper's enthusiasm. By the time we returned to the Ville and returned the bikes to the local vendor, I could barely walk and sitting down was a lousy alternative. I found out later from Thumper that we had ridden over 30 miles out and back. I was sore for several days following this excursion, and I never suggested that we do it again. We did make several more rides over the summer, but I insisted that they be shorter and on paved roads.

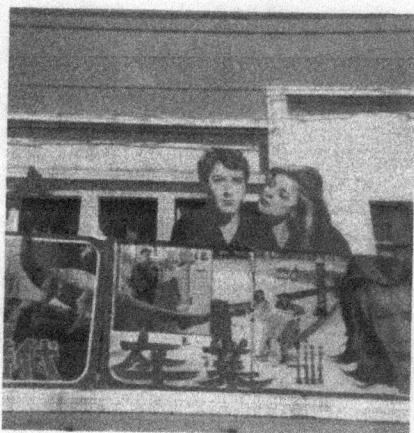

CHAPTER TWENTY-TWO:

The Secretary of the Army Comes for a Visit

One of the true highlights of my short military career occurred on May 23, 1972. Robert Froehlke, Secretary of the Army, made a visit to our Battalion for an inspection of our defense capabilities. Thumper and I were assigned to his entourage to cover his stay for *The Gauntlet*. I was given the task of interviewing him and covering his activities. Thumper came along as the resident photographer for the Battalion. We were given a Jeep to use for this event, and we followed along in the parade of vehicles that traveled with the Secretary wherever he went. There were several high-ranking military people there. They were mostly generals from the 38th Brigade and 8th U. S. Army, as well as a lot of security people. Thumper and I fully enjoyed being in the parade. Because we were reporting on the event we were allowed to be near the Secretary wherever he went. With Thumper snapping pictures, I was allowed to meet the Secretary and spend a few minutes with him for an interview. I thought this was pretty neat considering that I was just a draftee and didn't want to spend my whole life in the military.

The Secretary and his entourage traveled to Bravo Battery on the DMZ. It was at this site that I got my first view of how really serious all of this military stuff was in the realm of world politics and relations between different countries. There we were standing on our Tach site at Bravo Battery, and just across the valley were the North Koreans standing on their anti-aircraft Battery. We were close enough to the enemy to see them walking the perimeter of their defense without the use of binoculars. Our HAWK missiles were on their launchers facing north and were ready to fire, and their anti-aircraft guns were pointing south, also ready to fire. It was a scary sight to say the least. We were close enough to the other hill that we could see the barrels of their guns with the naked eye.

Later in the tour we were given a demonstration of how the guard dogs were trained to attack intruders. Every Battery in the Battalion had several guard dogs to help guard the perimeters of the Tach site. These dogs were the biggest dogs I have ever seen. They were a special breed of German shepherds that weighed at least 200 pounds. When the trainers had them stand them up on their hind legs they were at least 6 feet tall. Most of the dogs' handlers were very large guys, but the dogs they were training easily overpowered these guys when they were in attack mode. I was certainly impressed.

The whole scene was very surreal in a way. It was so quiet and hushed on these defense sites that you could hear a pin drop. You could almost hear the enemy talking to each other and they were several hundred yards away. Everyone talked in hushed voices, and there was tension in the air the whole time we were there. The security detail surrounding the Secretary of the Army was on alert for anything, and they never stopped scanning the perimeter of the Tach site during our entire stay.

The Secretary made his rounds talking with the soldiers and shaking hands and smiling in a political manner. Here he was walking around like he was at a garden party meeting his guests, and everybody surrounding him for security purposes was on their guard with scowls on their faces. It was just like in the movies and the news reels from World War II.

I did enjoy the experience though. It was a once-in-a-lifetime event. I was able to spend a full day hobnobbing with some of the Army's top brass. I ate the best food that the Army could produce, and I shook hands with one of the top guys in the U.S. Government. I considered it a rare privilege to be at this event. Since I was an ordinary drafted soldier with no aspirations of becoming a full-time soldier, it was pretty cool to be among the few selected to accompany the Secretary on his tour.

After returning to Camp Red Cloud, Thumper and I got together to formulate the article and the pictures he had taken to send down to Brigade for the newspaper. The story appeared in the following month's issue, and it was a full four-page feature with my byline and everything. The story must have been fairly well-written because a condensed version of it made it to the Army's *Pacific Stars and Stripes* newspaper later in the month. This represented my first published writing outside of the numerous articles I wrote in college. I still have a couple copies of the article among my mementos and personal treasures. Unfortunately, a lot of this sort of thing was lost a number of years ago when I was involved in a tornado that struck the town I was living in at the time.

Army Secretary

Visits B/2/71

POHWON-NI-Most batteries in the 38th Air Defense Artillery Brigade have one major role-protecting the skies over the Korean peninsula from hostile air attacks.

However Bravo 2/71 acquired another role for a short time late last month-entertaining the Secretary of the Army, the Honorable Robert F. Froehlke.

The Secretary flew in by helicopter and stepped out onto Bravo's TAC Site, amidst Alpha Launcher Section's missile salutes. BG Ernst E. Roberts, Brigade commanding general, was on hand to meet the Secretary and welcome him to the Brigade.

After a brief walk up the site, General Roberts briefed the Secretary

on the mission of the Brigade. Roberts showed that despite critical shortages in personnel, the Brigade has maintained a high degree of tactical readiness.

During the general's introduction, Secretary Froehlke asked about the personnel problems and living conditions of the troops here.

He learned that the average Air Defense soldier works a 10-12 hour schedule, six days a week. Most personnel in the Army today are now working a 5-day a week schedule. Mr. Froehlke learned first-hand that the nature of Air Defense requires long hours and a very demanding schedule.

Following the commanding ge-

Continued on Page 3

BG Ernst E. Roberts, 38th Brigade commanding general, briefs the Secretary of the Army Robert F. Froehlke and MG Winant Slide, Army chief of Information, on the mission of the Brigade at their quarters. (photo by De Young)

A model Hawk unit rolls by in March Order which prompted the Army Secretary to remark on the unusual size of the training aids.

After watching a brief demonstration of the Security Dogs, Mr. Froehlke looked at one of the well-padded trainers and said, 'Whatever we are paying you-it isn't enough!'

38th AIR DEFENSE ARTILLERY BDE

GAUNTLET

Vol. XI No. 11   OSAN AIR BASE   June 9, 1972

the man and the mission

Behind the scene

at Validation

Hawk Validation Firing is over. As reported in these pages in recent weeks, the firing exercise was conducted in a most successful manner.

The two Hawk batteries, Delta 2/71 and Delta 6/44, achieved the highest percentage of targets ever hit for tactically deployed units

anywhere in the world.

This week, SGT Robert A. Poindexter and photographer SP4 A.F. DeYoung take GAUNTLET readers behind the scene to meet some of the men who were responsible for this remarkable success. See Pages 4-5.

Army Secretary tours Bravo, 2/71

Continued from Page 1

neral's introduction, CPT Lawrence Brotherton II, Bravo battery commander, took over and gave the Secretary and his aides a detailed view of the battery itself.

Froehlke asked if the battery commander had any feelings on whether education has an important role in Air Defense jobs. The Bravo commander replied that education plays an important role in how well he performs.

The Secretary then learned how Hawk units are completely mobile and can be moved in total to another site at any time. As a model Hawk unit in March Order, rolled past the seated dignitaries, Mr. Froehlke remarked that the various pieces of equipment made rather large "training aids!"

The Army Secretary toured the TAC Site, asking the men whether they were Draftees or Careerists, how they liked it in Korea and how the Army was treating them.

After watching a brief demonstration of the Security Dogs, he

looked at one of the well-padded trainers and said, "Whatever we are paying you-it isn't enough!"

At the conclusion of the tour, Secretary Froehlke gave a short speech and held a question and answer session. He explained that he would like to have more dependents over here, but he could not foresee the Army having the funds nor the facilities in the near future to accomplish this program.

He asked how many men liked what they are doing and received a great outburt of laughter from the audience. He was then asked about the credibility of the JUMPS Pay System. He said the Army still believes that JUMPS is a sound system, but it needs some more "ironing out." He sympathized with those who are having pay problems here in Korea.

The Secretary of the Army left the men at Bravo with these thoughts: He believes that the Army's primary mission is that of PEACE and he, as Secretary of the Army, is doing all that he can to keep PEACE as the Primary Mission. He said he wants men to have "fun" while they

work and serve their country. Army Personnel in Korea may not always have fun while they work, but the men at Bravo 2/71 were lucky enough to be able to take a

little time out of their busy schedules to have some fun and relaxation with somebody from home who is "proud to be their boss!"

——Robert Poindexter——

BG Ernst Roberts briefs the Secretary of the Army and his party.

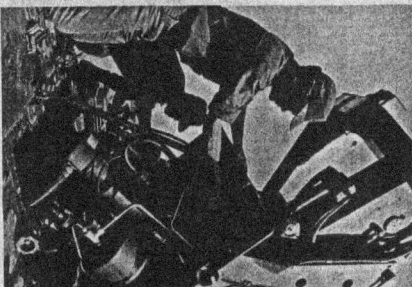

Delta men put validity into Sea Range Validation

**Story by
Robert
Poindexter**

**Photos by
A.F. DeYoung**

Hawk Validation is now
first firing, completed by
Delta 2/71, ends a two-month
program designed to evaluate
the Hawk missile system and
its support equipment.

The Validation Firing was

split into two phases. Delta
6/44 opened the exercise in
Phoenix, Arizona, and completed the firing with Phase
II.

The two Hawk batteries
compiled a .71 per cent kill
ratio. This was the highest

percentage of targets hit
ever achieved by tactically
deployed troops anywhere
up in all areas of the Hawk
system.

The Missile Assembly Crew
was trained intensively under
Annual Service Practice (Annual)...

voiced by the Equipment Maintenance Officer

The Firing Crew can
monthly checks on all the
equipment is better functionally checks on all the
hardware and to gain the
needed efficiency to pass
the validation.

The Firing Crew, can
perform various kinds of
training and those...

SP4 Robert P. Warren, fire control crewman, and SSG Donald Norton, crew chief of the
Hi Power Illuminator Radar (HPIR),
make a daily check on the
tactical generator, upper far right.

SP4 Kenneth G. Chambers, power generator operator, checks part of the

SP4 L/4 E. Eninger, missile crewman,
works on the launcher with the miniature
missile simulator center far right.

SPS David S. Ross, missile launcher mechanic, sets in the azimuth cutout clips in the
launcher, below.

SGT Larry W. Baker, fire control crewman,
aligns the HPIR, right.

PFC William H. Hedrick, from the
EMBO section, removes a fuze through the
simulator, lower far right.

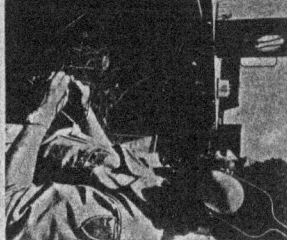

CHAPTER TWENTY-THREE:

SP/5 Promotion, The Defense Plan, and My Last First Sergeant

By June 1972, I was well-settled in as one of the tenured clerks in the Battalion. I was a SP/4 in rank with Acting Sergeant stripes on my fatigues. I was the sole clerk in the Orderly Room due to a reduction of forces in Korea. I was also serving as the Battery Orientation NCO and the Battalion Public Information Clerk. My numerous duties often had me working Monday through Friday and usually a half-day on Saturday.

At about this time, I was again ready for a promotion to a full-fledged SP/5 NCO. Unfortunately, I couldn't type my own promotion papers for this one. This promotion had to come from Battalion. I had to take a formal Promotion Board exam before I could receive it. At this point I only had a few months left to go in the Army, and the only real incentive to getting promoted was the slight increase in pay every month and the ability to ship more weight in goods home when I was ready to leave the country. After all, for the past several months I had been running the Orderly Room by myself wearing Sergeant's stripes and answering the phone as if I was the First Sergeant himself. Getting the actual promotion was not going to change my status that much anyway.

In other words, I was taking kind of a lazy approach to this whole thing and I didn't put that much effort into seeing that I was promoted. It was actually my own First Sergeant and Battery Commander who recommended me for the promotion in the first place. They were insisting that I go before the Promotion Board. How could I refuse to comply with their orders? They both did warn me, however, that my chances for promotion were slim on the first try because there were only a couple of these per month to hand out. But they both wanted my name among the mix of candidates so that I would be an almost shoe-in for the following month's Board. Their rationale on all of this had to do with the fact that they would be rotating out in the near future, and since they were so pleased with my work as the chief cook and bottle-washer for the Battery, they thought I deserved to be promoted to the elite status of SP/5. Who was I to argue with this kind of endorsement? Besides, I had a few more things that I wanted to purchase while I was still in the Army, and the extra pay would come in handy.

As expected I did not get the promotion on the first try, but I was basically informed by the First Sergeant that I had just missed it by a few promotion points. With one more month as a SP/4, I would have no trouble getting the promotion on the next Board of Review. I was promoted the following month, and the First Sergeant and the Battery Commander made a big production of the pinning ceremony. They even took me out to lunch at the Officer's Mess Hall. I took all of this in stride, and while I was happy with the promotion my only real thoughts were on the fact that I was starting to get "short" and I was looking forward to going home to the United States. This Army life was OK, but it was starting to get to be a drag since I had no plans for re-enlisting. I was ready to get on with my life and find out what I really wanted to do once I was back in the States.

As I have mentioned before, for several months I was the only clerk in the Orderly Room. The cutbacks in the Army's personnel at that time had caused many of us to take on additional duties. I had several titles and wore many hats, so to speak, during these months. On one hot and sultry Friday afternoon the Battery Commander came out of his office and asked what I had going on for the next couple of Saturdays. Since I could not think of anything pressing at the time, I said "nothing special." He informed me that he had a special project that he was working on and that if I didn't mind, he would like me to come in for a few hours the next

174

couple of Saturdays to assist him with it. He was rather vague as to what exactly we would be doing but that it was extremely important. Staying on the good side of the Battery Commander always had its benefits, so I agreed to donate a couple of my Saturdays to this unknown project.

The next morning I met the Battery Commander at the Orderly Room at around 8:00 a.m. When I walked into his office I found him mulling over several detailed charts and maps. His first question was about what kind of security clearance I had. I told him that I had received a "secret" clearance because of the nature of the paperwork I often was required to type. I cut orders and typed up all of the discipline letters and orders for the Battery as part of my duties as the Morning Report Clerk. He then told me that as of now I had a "top secret" clearance, at least for the next couple of weeks.

I was slightly apprehensive at this point as to what exactly we were about to do. He very calmly proceeded to tell me that he and I were about to rewrite the Battery's defense plan in case we were ever attacked by North Korea. To say the least, I was floored by this proclamation. Here I was, a drafted, newly promoted SP/5 Orderly Room clerk about to sit down with the Battery Commander and figure out the best way to retreat from our present location in Korea to a new location in case of an attack from the north. I thought I was dreaming!

I kept wondering why he had selected me for this task instead of the logical choice—the First Sergeant. He must have noticed my questioning look regarding all of this stuff. He went on to explain to me that since I had been in the Battery the longest of almost anyone and I had knowledge of all the personnel and detachments in the Battery, I was the only logical choice to assist him with re-writing the defense plan for the Battery. He further explained that he was relying on my knowledge of the local roads and streets surrounding Camp Red Cloud to formulate the best way to get out of Uijongbu in a hurry.

I never thought that my intimate knowledge of the Ville would ever come in handy for anything other than extracurricular activities. He also pointed out that he trusted me to keep this information under-my-hat, so to speak. This was one of those things that was to stay confidential. I took all of this as a vote of confidence in my abilities as a clerk in the

Orderly Room. I felt privileged to be trusted that much with material and knowledge that most guys in the Battery knew nothing about.

As it turned out, the next couple of weekends were pretty interesting. I learned a lot about military tactics and so forth that I would have otherwise never known about. A couple of nice lunches with the Battery Commander didn't hurt anything either. With all of this added responsibility, I was gaining an almost "carte blanche" status in the Orderly Room. Whenever I needed something or wanted to do something I simply had to ask the Battery Commander for his approval. He very rarely said no to anything I requested. This fact would become invaluable upon the arrival of the incoming First Sergeant.

One of the items that the Battery Commander and I went over during these planning meetings was the order in which various units and vehicles were to leave the area in our tactical retreat. We were going over this plan when I asked the obvious question: "Where did the Battery Commander and his loyal Morning Report Clerk fit into this parade?" After a brief chuckle, the Battery Commander stated that we would be in the first Jeep leaving the Post. He also pointed out that I would have to be in his Jeep to maintain communications with the other detachments and vehicles. Besides, he said, "Someone has to keep track of the casualties!"

I was having a great time with all of this until he said that. The prospect of being in a situation where someone might actually get killed or wounded was still a rather foreign idea to me, even after being in the military for a while now. At this late stage in my brief Army career I was still guilty of not taking all of this Army stuff too seriously. After all, I was a clerk!

By the middle of July1972, I was breaking-in my third First Sergeant and my fourth Battery Commander at Headquarters Battery, 2nd, 71st, ADA. As had been the case before, we were going through a transition period of getting used to each other regarding their expectations of me and me of them. Getting along with Battery Commanders was not a problem since I didn't directly work for them on a day-to-day basis. Most of my work went through the First Sergeant and then on to the Battery Commander. I typed letters and such for both of my bosses, but most everything I did was reviewed by the First Sergeant. I would take some things directly to the Battery Commander for approval depending on the nature of the paperwork.

Every First Sergeant I worked for had a different management style, so getting used to their little quirks and pet peeves took some time. The two previous First Sergeants were really pretty cool guys, and they pretty much left everything up to me in terms of organizing the office and determining the priorities on the paperwork that had to be done. The new First Sergeant was a different breed of cat, however. He was a micro-manager. Everything had to go through him and he was really a stickler for details.

My typing skills, for the most part, were really pretty good. I also thought that since I was the only one in the office with a degree in journalism that no one should be questioning my use of the English language. I had been proofreading letters written by the First Sergeants and Battery Commanders the entire time I had been in the Orderly Room. I often had to correct their spelling and grammar. It was not uncommon for me to completely change the way they had written something before I typed everything in its final draft. Re-typing things was one of my pet peeves. I didn't like typing things over and over again just because the letter writer had an afterthought after the letter had been typed to perfection.

As you might imagine, after running the office pretty much the way I wanted to for several months and then to have someone come in and start changing everything I was doing and questioning everything I did didn't sit well with me. The First Sergeant and I started clashing right from the beginning. At first I sloughed most of it off and tried to get along with this jerk. But the further things went along the worse it got. He was even questioning my organization of the office, and this was just a couple of months past our annual General Inspection in which I had received rave reviews from the inspectors for my organizational skills. Besides, I was getting "short," I still didn't have a replacement, and I really didn't give a flying you-know-what where this guy was coming from. All I wanted to do was coast along and get out of the Army as soon as possible.

Things got so bad that the First Sergeant would come in and not even acknowledge that I was already there at work. He would drop work in my inbox and not even say anything. This included anything that he thought needed changing, including the changes I had made in his original work.

It really got silly after a while. After a couple of weeks of this I decided that something had to be done about this idiot.

One afternoon I found myself alone in the office with just the Battery Commander in the next room. The First Sergeant was out for the day on some errand, and I found this to be a convenient time to discuss my situation with his boss. Yes I was going around the chain-of-command but I was desperate! I still had another month-and-a-half to go before leaving the country. I wanted to keep my newly acquired rank and pay. If things didn't improve soon I was probably going to tell the First Sergeant where he could put all of his stupid ideas! I decided that I would find a way to get around this guy without getting in trouble and receiving disciplinary action. I was sure that he was about to write me up for insubordination in the line of duty. We obviously had a personality conflict on just about everything we did or said to each other.

I knocked on the Battery Commander's door and asked if he had a few minutes to talk. He said that he did, so I proceeded to inform him of my situation with the new First Sergeant. I was pretty candid about it, and I basically told him that I didn't mind doing my job and that I would continue to do it to the best of my abilities. I told him that the First Sergeant and I were not getting along, and that he was really starting to hassle me about everything I did. I basically said that if the First Sergeant didn't leave me alone I was going to let the paperwork pile up to the ceiling of the Orderly Room. I also mentioned that I was going to be leaving in about 45 days and no one had mentioned anything about getting a replacement for my job. Apparently, the First Sergeant had failed to mention this to the Battery Commander in their numerous discussions. The Battery Commander assured me that he would take this up with the First Sergeant as soon as he could, and he advised me to continue as I saw fit as to the paperwork and organization of the office. He told me that the previous Battery Commander had given me a high recommendation on my work and skills, and that he presently did not have a problem with what I was doing.

The following morning I was hard at work when the Battery Commander called the First Sergeant into his office and shut the door. As far as I could remember, this was the first time in the past year in the Orderly Room that this had ever happened. I could not hear the conversation going on in the other room but there was an occasional raised voice, mostly coming from the First Sergeant. The meeting lasted about 30 minutes, and when the First Sergeant came back out in the Orderly Room I could tell that he was not very happy. However, from that point forward until I left for the United States the First Sergeant left me alone. In fact, the following day he told me to start looking for my replacement among the incoming personnel. A while later, he told me to find two guys instead of one. So I began the process of finding my new "turtles" to train in the jobs connected with the Orderly Room.

By the 20th of July 1972, I had found two men to replace me in the Orderly Room. The First Sergeant left it up to me to pick them out and train them in the way I saw fit. As it turned out, I picked my replacements the same way that I had been picked. I called a friend in Personnel down at Brigade and told him that I needed a couple of guys for the Orderly Room. They both needed to type and have somewhat of a college education. He started going over the incoming manifests for arrivals in Korea and found a generator operator and a HAWK Missile Launcher Crewman who fit my requirements.

Neither of these guys had the slightest idea they were going to be clerks until they came into the Orderly Room. As it turned out, they were both real sharp kids and really fast learners. Within two weeks time I had them doing most of the work in the Orderly Room. I would just review their work before putting it into the First Sergeant's inbox. I used this time to catch up on correspondence and filing. I had let most of the filing go for a while since I was the only one in the Orderly Room, and I almost never had time to do any of it anyway. Even though I couldn't stand the First Sergeant I felt it wouldn't be fair to leave his office in a mess when I left the country. What he did with the organization after I left I could care less about, but I kept it all straight until then.

I had my own way of taunting the First Sergeant as the days passed into August 1972. As I mentioned, my two replacements caught on to their new assignments rather quickly. I had one of them concentrating on the Morning Report, while the other one took on cutting orders and typing letters, etc. I still handled the orientations for the new arrivals, as well as the coordination with the other sections in the Battalion on the processing-in procedures. This involved walking the new people around the Battalion offices and getting them settled into their respective Batteries and job assignments. This got me out of the office quite a bit of the time, so the First Sergeant and I managed to tolerate each other for the rest of the time I was in Korea.

I also had my duties as the Battalion Public Information Clerk, and I occasionally had to go out to cover events for the newspaper.

By the time that I was down to about two weeks to go before leaving the country, I began coming in later in the morning to check on my replacements. I would stick around for an hour or two to make sure they were lined up on their work for the day and then I would take off for extended lunch breaks. I knew that the First Sergeant wasn't thrilled about this but he never said anything since all of the work was getting done in a timely fashion. I made sure that the typing was error-free, and in some cases I re-typed stuff myself to keep him satisfied. We got along OK, but you could tell that it was a stiff relationship.

The First Sergeant did his work and I did mine. We were never buddies. I had the advantage in one respect though. I knew where everything was in the office and I knew all of the personnel in the Battery and the Battalion. The First Sergeant was forced to depend on me to get things done and to contact different sections and detachments in the Battalion. In the end, he did thank me for my help in the Orderly Room. After all, I left him and his two new clerks in pretty good shape when I left the country.

CHAPTER TWENTY-FOUR:

The Arrival of Sugar Bear and My Meeting With the Battalion XO

One of the many highlights of my tour in Korea was the arrival of one of my former D.I.'s from Fort Bliss, Texas. As you will recall, a bunch of my friends and I decided to test out the new Army policy on moustaches and how long you could grow them. This infuriated our D.I. at the time. I am sure that our defiance of the policy had cost all of us a promotion to PFC out of AIT. It was our conclusion that our loveable Sugar Bear had been the guy who had made sure that we were not promoted. While we were disappointed at the time for not getting promoted, we also understood that we had pushed the limits of Sugar Bear's patience. Besides, we had gotten a lot of laughs in our off-time over the whole situation.

I was at my desk in the Orderly Room one day when to my great surprise, my old buddy Sugar Bear walked in to process into the Battalion. He had just rotated in from Fort Bliss to do a 13-month hitch in Korea. I'm not sure who was more surprised when he first recognized me as he walked in. He started to say hello, and then he realized that I was no longer one of his trainees but a three-striper Sergeant. He stumbled over his greeting, apparently having a great deal of difficulty with calling me "Sergeant." You could see the obvious surprise in his face. I being a cool guy and all, I diplomatically greeted him in my best Orderly Clerk fashion. I welcomed him to the Battalion and gave him the normal orientation spiel that I gave all the new guys coming into the country. I never gave him a clue that I was as surprised as he was at seeing him show up in Korea, much less in our location. I did my administrative duties with his records, recorded his name for the roster, and then sent him on his way through the rest of the Battalion offices.

I patiently waited until he was out of the Orderly Room before I made my first phone call to my buddies over at Battalion and Personnel. Did I have a deal for him!

After a few short calls in which I explained what had happened to me at AIT with the good Sergeant, I successfully had him shipped to our most remote line Battery in the Battalion. He was about to spend the next 13 months in the middle of nowhere!

This particular line Battery was so remote in its location that it didn't even have a large village connected with it. It was right on the DMZ and in the middle of the mountains. I couldn't think of a better place to send him so that he could reflect on his misdeeds while at Fort Bliss.

All of this went on unbeknownst to him, which made it more satisfying to me. I was so proud of myself at getting the good Sergeant back for not promoting me out of AIT that I even contacted my cohorts in crime from Fort Bliss to give them the good news. Once again, we all got a good laugh or two at Sugar Bear's expense. I was not normally a vindictive guy, but this was one of those times when I couldn't resist the temptation to mess with somebody. I have been known over the years to be a bit of a pot-stirrer. I have always had my own unique way of evening the score, so to speak. Being of small stature, I have run into many situations when others have messed with me for one thing or another. Brute strength not being one of my assets in life, it has never worked so I have been forced to use my brain in these situations. Fortunately God provided me with one.

Some people refer to this as having a "Napoleon complex." We shorter people have a tendency to be more aggressive and try harder than others to stay up with the group. I have to admit that when I was younger, I was pretty feisty at times. I had gone through high school and college taking a lot of shit from the big guys almost on a daily basis. By the time I had reached my early 20's I had perfected several methods at getting back at people for their misdeeds. I simply used my intelligence to return the favor. Most of the time the payback was so subtle that the intended individual never realized what had happened to him until much later, and by then they couldn't prove that I was the culprit.

I have always lived by a simple code that I have developed over the years. I simply apply the code of a privateer. I have always been fascinated with the many accounts in history of such famous pirates as Blackbeard. I have often thought that if I could have lived at another time in history, I would have liked living during the time of the swashbucklers or around the time of the American Revolution. I have always thought that this was a time of great excitement in our short history as a country. It would have been great to be around the likes of Benjamin Franklin, Patrick Henry, George Washington, and Thomas Jefferson. These people were visionaries who made up the fabric that has evolved into what makes the United States the great country that it is today.

One of the most famous privateers in history was a fellow named Sir Francis Drake. I do believe in my studies of the man that he was actually a pirate. The only difference with him was that he did a lot of his pirating under the auspices and blessings of the Queen of England. As long as he shared his spoils with Mother England, he was allowed to operate as a pirate. He became very famous and very wealthy at the expense of France and Spain during those days. He simply took advantage of the fact that the Queen of England knew what he was doing and refused to have him punished for his crimes as long as he shared his booty with her. He pirated for several years under this arrangement.

My code in life is much like Sir Francis Drake's. I simply have taken advantage of situations that have presented themselves. My situation with Sugar Bear is a good example of this. Here I was the Battery Clerk at Headquarters with an enormous amount of influence throughout the Battalion as to where people were assigned for duty stations. I simply made use of my position to see that Sugar Bear spent the next 13 months in oblivion in lovely Korea. After all, he was the one who decided that I should go another two months on the meager pay of an E-2 trainee not me! I wasn't mad at him—I just wanted to get even.

You see, that's the difference between a pirate and a privateer. A pirate rapes, pillages, and plunders. A privateer simply pillages and plunders. He has ethics. Thinking along these terms, I could have done a lot worse to my old buddy besides send him to the Battery from hell. I could have made sure that my friends in Personnel lost all of his records or worse yet, lost his shot record. Those two things were among the worst that could happen to you while in a foreign country. If your records came up missing you could spend weeks waiting for them to materialize again. Worse yet, you had to retake all of those immunizations again before you left the country. I thought the only ethical thing to do was send him into oblivion.

I was rolling along toward getting out of Korea in fine shape. I had a couple of guys working for me in the Orderly Room, I was getting along with the First Sergeant, and the newest Battery Commander thought I was the best thing since apple pie was invented since I had an answer for most of his questions concerning things about the Battery and its personnel. I was catching up with a pile of letters that I had let go for a while that I needed to get out in the mail before I left the country. Most of these letters involved indebtedness by some of the present personnel in the Battery. Some were even about guys who were no longer in the Battery or had left Korea entirely. This was a tedious process because you had to track down where these guys were and then write letters to various people or Companies that were looking for them to collect bills that they had skipped out on.

One of the tricks that an amazing amount of guys had employed was to get married to one of the local girls in Korea. Some even decided for God-knows-what- reason to stay in Korea after their enlistments had expired. During my short stay in Korea I had seen very little that would entice me to actually live in this country for any great length of time. I was in Korea for only one reason: because the Army, in all of its wisdom, had sent me there. Some of these guys had actually taken up residence in Korea. Finding out where people live in a foreign country and getting their correct addresses was sometimes a real adventure.

One morning I was hard at work writing and typing these letters when I received a very strange phone call. It was the Command Sergeant Major for the Battalion. I was informed that the Battalion Executive Officer wanted to see me in his office right after lunch. I couldn't for the life of me figure out what he wanted to see me about. After all, I had been pretty busy of late training my replacements on the procedures in the Orderly Room and so forth. I hadn't been on any recent escapades in the Ville. I had been generally behaving myself like most guys did when they were getting close to leaving the country. Therefore, I could not think of anything that a Major would need to see me about.

Now I was no stranger to talking with officers. I encountered them almost on a daily basis. There were local officers in the Battery or on the Post most of the time . I never had extended conversations with any of them though. You would usually only cross paths with them in your travels around the Post going to the Mess Hall or the PX. When you passed near them on the sidewalk or the street, it was a generally accepted practice to greet them with a salute acknowledging their rank and a simple "Good morning" or "Good afternoon, sir." This was one of the many drills that had been driven into our heads as early as my first couple of days in the Service. You were required to be respectful of officers at all times—even if they were idiots. In most cases, these officers were lower-ranked lieutenants or captains. The chances of running into higher-ranked officers were pretty slim. We enlisted guys didn't travel in the same circles with these guys, if you know what I mean. So having to talk with a Major was a pretty big deal. Usually this meant that you were in trouble for some reason or another. Since I couldn't think of anything that I needed to be worried about I had no idea why the Battalion XO needed to see me.

Promptly at 1300 hours, I arrived at the Battalion offices and reported to the CSM. He escorted me to the Battalion XO's office and announced my arrival. After giving him the mandatory salute and so forth, the Major asked me to sit down. We began the conversation with him asking me how I was doing. He alluded to the fact that I was getting "short" in my tour in Korea. We went over what my plans were in my return to civilian life. I basically had no real plan other than returning home and deciding what to do with the rest of my life. I had a job waiting for me on the railroad since I had been drafted into the Army, but I wasn't entirely sure that was what I really wanted to do for a career. I had some thoughts of trying to pursue a career in the newspaper or advertising business, but beyond that things were pretty wide open. Marriage was a remote possibility since I didn't have any girlfriends waiting for me at home. The Major wished me well in whatever I decided to do with the rest of my life.

We also went over my records of promotion while in Korea and discussed my numerous duties and jobs I had done for the Battery and Battalion in the past year or so. For the most part, we simply reviewed everything in my personnel file. At the time I thought maybe this was a normal thing that happened when you were about to leave the Army. They wanted to make sure that all of the information in your file was correct before you returned to the States and civilian life. As I would find out later after returning to civilian status, I had been recommended by one of my Battery Commanders to receive the Army Commendation Medal for my work in the Orderly Room and my role as Battalion Public Information Clerk. Apparently, my meeting with the Major had a lot more meaning than I realized at the time. He was actually interviewing me as part of the process for my receiving this award. I actually didn't receive the medal and the commendation letter until I had been back home for a couple of months. Connecting the two events never occurred to me until much later in my life though.

Before we finished our conversation, the Major made an astounding prediction about my future. He predicted that within a very short amount of time after I returned to civilian life that I would probably be married and that I would decide fairly quickly what I wanted to do for a living. How he had arrived at these conclusions I had no idea. I left his office thinking that he was some kind of a nut case. How in the world could this Major who barely knew who I was come up with a prediction like that? Like I said, I had no girlfriend at home and no prospects of meeting one. And as to my future in the work world, the conclusions were even more vague and cloudy than my love life. While I walked back to the Orderly Room I shook my head several times thinking about what the Major had said. At that time I just wrote all of this off as a fluke. He had no more of an idea of what my future held than I did.

Later that same day, my buddy Thumper and I got together at the NCO Club. We were talking about the events of the day. After several drinks, we both came to the conclusion that the Major was just making conversation and that he was full of shit about my future. We were so convinced of this that we made a deal between the two of us that whoever got married first after returning to civilian life had to buy the other guy a quart of his favorite booze. Thumper's choice was Jack Daniels, and my choice was Chivas Regal. The winner of the bet had to travel to the other guy's wedding. We both thought that we had plenty of time before any of this would occur. Getting married at any time in the near future was a remote possibility for either one of us.

As it turned out, I ended up losing the bet. After returning to civilian life I took a cruise to the Bahamas with my parents and I met my future first wife on that cruise. We were engaged by Christmas of that year, and we were married by the following May. Thumper did come to the wedding from California and he did a lot of our photography as a wedding gift. It's funny how things that you do in jest come back to haunt you when you least expect them to. All along, I thought that this was one of the surest bets I had ever made. I was sure that Thumper would get married first and that I would get a fun trip to Los Angeles out of the deal.

CHAPTER TWENTY-FIVE:

My Last Month in Korea and the Last Hurrah

By mid-August 1972, I was really getting "short." I had under 30 days left to go in my tour in Korea. Things were going well in the Orderly Room. My two replacements were really getting into the swing of things. They were doing so well that I was able to spend less and less time overseeing their activities. This also meant that I had to spend less time around the new First Sergeant. As I have already mentioned, we were not exactly the best of friends. He was in charge of the office, but I was the one who was seeing that the work got done. This system worked relatively well, and I tried to see that my replacements did the work to suit him. After all, I was leaving in a month so it didn't really make a hill of beans difference to me what they did after I left. I had been left to do things using my own system for nearly a year, so it was time to hand everything over to someone else.

I used my extra time to begin my preparations for leaving Korea. I started to pack my numerous acquisitions while in Korea and Japan. I had acquired a new stereo system, including a reel-to-reel tape deck, turntable, two amplifiers, and two very large Sansui speakers. I also picked up a very nice Yashica 35-millimeter camera with two extra lenses and a tripod. I had picked up some civilian clothes too. Plus, I had all of the stuff that had been sent to me in care packages from home.

There was the infamous popcorn popper that we had used for many purposes during the past 12 months. I had also accumulated a baseball glove, a couple of windbreakers from our golf team, and of all things, a handmade smoking jacket that I used to wear a lot in my off-time. And then there was the clothing that the Army had issued me in Basic Training. When it came time to ship all of this stuff home, it came to an amazing 480 pounds. I was allowed to ship 500 pounds as a Specialist 5- ranked enlisted man.

During my last month in Korea, I also began making contacts with my friends in Personnel at Brigade to ensure that I left Korea on time. You had to pretty much arrange this stuff yourself. After a few calls to the right places I was relatively sure that I would not have to spend any extra time in this God-forsaken country than I had to. I was slated to leave on September 13th, 1972. This being my birthday made things all the more sweet. I couldn't think of a better birthday present than to leave a place that I had no love for and was forced to stay in for over a year. It was almost like getting out of jail.

I have never been in a place other than Korea that has such extremes in weather. I had gone from monsoons to oppressive heat and humidity to freezing cold and back to monsoons in a year's time. There were a few nice weeks in the spring and fall, but otherwise the weather was a little too dicey for my taste. Living around Chicago most of my life, I have seen some really crummy weather at times, but the weather in Korea makes the weather in Chicago look balmy. I was glad to be going back to more tolerable conditions.

My last hurrah in Korea took place during my last week in the country. There was a tradition at Headquarters Battery 2nd, 71st, ADA for outgoing guys. Each guy leaving was treated to a going away party by all of his friends and co-workers. One of the gifts presented to each guy was a pewter tankard with our unit's logo on it. It was engraved with the nicknames of all of his friends on it too. The only catch in all of this was that after being presented with this tankard, each guy had to decide what he wanted to drink from it during the party. His friends would then proceed to make sure that this tankard was never empty until the party was over. Needless to say, each departing G.I. was rendered completely useless by the end of the festivities. That was the whole purpose of the party in the first place!

This was one last chance for your buddies to get you completely stinko before you left the country. Since drinks at the NCO Club were only 25 cents, for a few dollars' donation you could have one hell of a party!

Finally, it was my turn for the "Last Rights Ceremony." We called it that because in some cases we weren't sure if the outgoing man was going to survive the party or not. More than one of them had to be escorted back to their barracks. After receiving double and triple shots of the chosen poison for several hours navigation to anywhere was impossible. Walking around a Post full of drainage ditches created to run-off monsoon rains could be dangerous for someone with obvious navigational deficiencies. After all, we just made sure they were good and drunk—not hurt. That could delay their departure from good old Korea.

It was now my turn. I had acquired over the past year a taste for Black Russians. I felt that this would be a decent drink to sip on all evening. I had attended several of these parties over the past year, and I had consumed several Black Russians over the course of these parties. I always managed to stay somewhat sober. I was often chosen to escort the departing G.I. to their assigned barracks because most everyone else was too drunk to do it themselves.

This strategy worked for *most* of my party. I managed to get through the first few hours without getting completely blitzed. However, my supposed friends seeing that I was not getting sufficiently drunk, employed some dastardly techniques to ensure that I was going to follow the tradition of Headquarters Battery 2nd, 71st, ADA. I was pretty far along toward drunken behavior after about four hours of drinking with no food to eat other than a few peanuts and pretzels at the bar. At some point that I really can't recall, my supposed friends decided that I should try another drink. They would not take no for an answer, and they provided me with some concoction that included sloe gin, vodka, and some sort of cherry-flavored liquor. After just a few sips of this stuff, I was heading for the bathroom to throw-up everything that I had consumed over the evening. I was sicker than a dog, and the room never stopped spinning from that point forward. Somehow I ended up back in my own bed in my own barracks though.

The next morning I could not remember anything from the night before other than the fact that I had been to a party in my honor. As you might guess, I was kidded a lot during my last days in Korea. There were also many tales going around the Battery about my escapades of that night. I am pretty sure that I really didn't do anything other than sleep off the booze. My buddies, of course, tried to convince me that I had run off to the Ville and run amok with the natives as part of my last fling in Korea. I denied everything of course!

CHAPTER TWENTY-SIX:

Time to Leave Korea and Say Goodbye to My Friends

As September 1, 1972 rolled around, I was down to less than two weeks left to go in Korea. At this time I was actively monitoring the progress of my orders and paperwork to return to the United States. I didn't want to spend any longer in Korea than was absolutely necessary. After all, you never knew when the North Koreans were going to start acting up. The last thing I wanted to have happen was an invasion by the North Koreans right about the time I was ready to leave the country. That could screw everything up! So I would call my friends down in Brigade Personnel every couple of days to see if they had any news on my transfer orders or if my name came up on any of the outgoing manifests. Each time I called they assured me that they were making every effort to get me out of Korea on time. In fact, they were so diligent in their efforts that they almost sent me home too soon.

You see, at this time the Army was downsizing its forces overseas with the hostilities in Vietnam winding down a little. The deal was that if you came back to the United States with less than 150 days to go in your obligation to serve in the Army, you were discharged early. My magic day was September 8, 1972. At that point I would have exactly 149 days left to go in my obligation. My buddies in Personnel got a little overzealous in their efforts to get me out of Korea and managed to get me on a manifest to leave the country on the 7th of September. One of the guys called me with the good news just after the Labor Day holiday. Now ordinarily I would have been thrilled to leave Korea a day sooner, but after I started counting the days I realized that they were sending me back to the States too soon for the 150- days-or-less discharge plan. I called this guy back right away in a panic. At first he thought I had gone mad. Here he had gone to all of the trouble to get me out of the country a day early, and now I was telling him to cancel the order.

After explaining my dilemma, he realized the mistake that had been made and said he would cancel the orders and reload the paperwork and run it through again. He told me that it might take a few days to straighten everything out and that I might get delayed in leaving the country. While I was not thrilled with this thought, I was willing to wait a few extra days to make sure that I was returning to the States with plenty of cushion on the 150-days-or less policy.

My last few days in Korea were kind of a drag because all of my personal belongings had already been shipped back to the United States. All I had left in my cubicle was my locker with my military work clothes and my dress uniform to go home in. I was forced to spend a lot of my off-time reading books and magazines in the Day Room, going to movies at the Post theater, or drinking myself silly at the NCO Club. I was avoiding visiting the Ville and messing around with the local girls. The last thing I needed to do was to contract some exotic disease during my last few days in this crazy place. I also used these few extra days to make the rounds visiting with my buddies in the Battery and Battalion offices. Most every evening was spent at the NCO Club having a few drinks with one or the other of my friends discussing what my plans were for civilian life.

Finally, a couple of days ahead of time I got the word that my orders were in at Brigade and I was listed on the manifest to leave the country on the 13th of September. I couldn't have received a better birthday present. I officially processed out of Headquarters Battery 2nd, 71st, ADA on the 12th of September, and I left Camp Red Cloud, Uijongbu, Korea for my departure location at an Air Force base in Pusan. It was raining the day I left for Pusan. This was also ironic since it was raining the day I had arrived in Korea. So my one lasting memory of Korea began and ended on the same note—torrential rain! Since I was leaving this time, I did not let this get me down.

I arrived in Pusan on the afternoon of the 12th, and after checking in with the Personnel people handling my departure from Korea I settled in at the temporary barracks provided for outgoing personnel. I met up with some guys who were leaving on the same day I was, and we went to the Mess Hall for dinner. We then spent the rest of the evening bull-shitting and playing cards. Then the morning of the 13th finally arrived. I was awake early in anxious anticipation of my final departure from Korea.

CHAPTER TWENTY-SEVEN:

The Flight Home and My Discharge From the Army

My flight from Pusan, Korea was scheduled for an 8:00 a.m. departure. I was heading back to the States on a direct flight to San Francisco. I was up early and was ready to go by 6:00 a.m. After grabbing some chow at the Mess Hall, I arrived at the assigned staging area for the bus ride to the airport. As usual in the Army, there I was in my fresh dress uniform standing in line to check in for the bus ride. Standing in lines had become a way of life for me during the past year-and-a-half. For the first time though, I didn't mind the wait. We soon boarded the bus for the ride to the airport terminal. Upon arriving at the airport terminal and checking in for the flight, I arrived at the waiting area. As was typical in the Army's way of doing things, everything was backed up and behind schedule.

As it turned out, I ended up waiting practically the whole day to leave Korea. It was late-afternoon on the 13th by the time the plane for our group of G.I.'s arrived at the airport. As the plane rolled up to the gate area I was astounded by the name on the side of the airplane. I knew ahead of time that we were traveling by a commercial airline back to the States. The name I saw on the plane just about floored me: Flying Tiger Airlines. I couldn't believe it. After surviving Basic Training, AIT, and 13 months in Korea, I was heading back to the United States on what looked like a 20-year-old jet owned by an airline company that I thought had gone out of existence during World War II! I was more than a little concerned by this development. I knew that our government was cheap but this was ridiculous. Flying Tiger Airlines? What happened to TWA, Braniff, United, or American?

In spite of my many reservations about the reliability and integrity of the air- worthiness of the airplane I was about to travel on, I boarded the plane anyway. I was ready to go and this appeared to be the only plane available. I said a little prayer as we took off for San Francisco. To this very day, I am not very comfortable with flying. If I have the time my first choice of travel is driving. I prefer to have complete control of my own destiny. I have flown many hundreds of hours at this point in my life, but I'm still not completely at ease until the airplane that I am traveling on lands at its destination. Fortunately, our flight of about 10 hours or so was uneventful. Our pilot gave us a smooth ride over the Pacific Ocean and we landed at the San Francisco International Airport. Since we had crossed the International Dateline while going over the Pacific, it was once again or still was the 13th of September.

After the overnight flight from Korea and being up for the better part of the past 30 hours or so, I was exhausted. My one consolation was that I was finally back in the good old United States of America! I could actually speak English again instead of the quasi Korean-English I had adopted for the past 13 months.

After getting off the plane and collecting my trusty duffle bag, I boarded a military bus for the hour-long ride to the U.S. Army Personnel Center in Oakland, California. It was now approaching the noon hour, and I was looking forward to another long afternoon of waiting in lines to process out of the Army. This process took a lot longer than I had anticipated. By the time I had gone through all of the different processing stations at the Personnel Center and picked up my travel orders and vouchers for the plane ride home to Chicago, it was after 6:00 p.m. I finally boarded another military bus and rode it back to the San Francisco International Airport. By the time I arrived there, I had already missed the last flight to Chicago for the day.

I called my parents for the first time in several months to let them know that I had arrived back in the States safe and sound. I only saw my parents three times in the 19 months that I was in the Army. They came down once during my Basic Training to see me graduate to Advanced Training. I also saw them for a week or so between Basic and Advanced Training. The last time I had seen them at this point was for a short time before I left for Korea. I also talked to them once on the phone while I was in Korea. Otherwise, you did all of your communicating through writing letters. During this most recent phone call, I told them the good news that as of 0001 hours on the 14th of September I would be a civilian again. They were disappointed that I had missed all of the flights to Chicago for the day, but they agreed to meet me upon my arrival in Chicago the next morning.

The following morning I caught a flight to Chicago. I was now a civilian, but since I still had my wrinkled travel uniform on I felt like I was in the Army. I was still in a daze from jet lag and crossing so many time zones. I was having trouble putting intelligent sentences together. Even ordering a simple soft drink from the extremely attractive flight attendant was a major challenge. She must have thought that I was suffering from battle fatigue or something. Feeling sorry for me, she was very attentive and checked to see that I was comfortable several times during the flight.

As I flew back to Chicago, I was thinking that getting back into the swing of things in civilian life was not going to be an easy transition. Nineteen months in the Army, including 13 months overseas, had significantly changed my perspective on things. I was now a 24-year-old man instead of the 22-year-old kid just out of college who had entered the Army. I had been through a lot of different situations and had seen how the other half of the world lives. I could think on my own, and I had a newfound confidence in myself. While in Korea, I had been in a position of authority and responsibility. I felt fully confident that I could determine my future on my own without relying on my parents to help me make decisions. I was ready for adulthood. I wasn't sure that they were ready for it though. Only time would tell.

I finally arrived at Chicago's O'Hare International Airport at around 10:00 a.m. on the 14th of September. I met my parents at the baggage claim where I retrieved my trusty duffle bag. I have to admit, in spite of my wrinkled travel uniform I had cut a pretty good figure of a chiseled soldier. I still had my moustache, and I looked like one tough little son of a bitch. I weighed in at a very trim 130 pounds. As usual, my mother was emotional and my father was stoic. I could tell that he was sizing me up with my new manly appearance. We had a lot to talk about, but now was not the time. "That Shade of Green" had taken its toll on all of us.

HEADQUARTERS, 38th ARTILLERY BRIGADE(AD)

APO San Francisco 96570

CITATION

THE ARMY COMMENDATION MEDAL

is awarded to

SPECIALIST FIVE ROBERT A. POINDEXTER

UNITED STATES ARMY

for

DISTINGUISHED AND EXCEPTIONALLY MERITORIOUS SERVICE DURING THE PERIOD 10 AUGUST 1971 TO 12 SEPTEMBER 1972. DURING THIS PERIOD SPECIALIST POINDEXTER SERVED AS BATTERY CLERK FOR HEADQUARTERS AND HEADQUARTERS BATTERY 2D BATTALION, 71ST AIR DEFENSE ARTILLERY. IN HIS CAPACITY AS BATTERY CLERK HE CONSISTENTLY DISPLAYED OUTSTANDING JOB KNOWLEDGE, INITIATIVE AND JUDGEMENT WHILE MAINTAINING A HIGH DEGREE OF ADMINISTRATIVE EFFICIENCY. HE HAS PROVED HIMSELF TO BE FULLY KNOW- LEDGEABLE OF ADMINISTRATIVE PROCEDURES. HIS OUTSTANDING EFFORT, INITIATIVE AND PROFESSIONALISM PLAYED A LARGE PART IN THE ORDERLY ROOM RECEIVING ONLY MINOR COMMENTS IN ADMINISTRATION DURING THE ANNUAL GENERAL INSPECTION. SPECIALIST POINDEXTER ACCEPTED ALL ADDITIONAL DUTIES WITH ZEAL AND ENTHUSIASM. ONE ADDITIONAL DUTY AS PUBLIC INFORMATION CLERK REQUIRED MANY OFF DUTY HOURS, IN WHICH HE VOLUNTEERED TO WRITE ARTICLES ON THE HAWK MISSILE SYSTEM, FOR PUBLICATION IN THE PACIFIC STARS AND STRIPES AND THE BRIGADE NEWSPAPER. SPECIALIST POINDEXTER'S EXCEPTIONAL PERFORMANCE IS IN KEEPING WITH THE HIGHEST TRADITION OF THE MILITARY SERVICE AND REFLECTS GREAT CREDIT UPON HIMSELF, HIS UNIT, AND THE UNITED STATES ARMY.

CHAPTER TWENTY-EIGHT:

Reflections

As I wrap up this project, I have recently finished a 38-year career with the Burlington Northern Railroad. I am loving retirement and am looking forward to possible literary pursuits. I have lived my life and have served my country. It has affected the way I look at things. I'm not saying the following comments are right or wrong—it's just how I feel now as a patriotic American.

I served a total of 19 months and six days on Active Duty in the United States Army. I have many fond memories and a few not-so-fond memories of that experience. Many of the things that I learned during my time in the Army have had a profound effect on how I do things today. How I view life in general and many of my daily habits all had their birth during those 19 months of my life.

When I was drafted into the Army in early 1971, I was starry-eyed, somewhat liberal, and idealistic. Outside of my limited time on my own living with my roommates at school, I didn't have the slightest idea about adulthood. At that time, I felt that there were no unsolvable problems. Everything had a simple solution. All you had to do was apply simple logic to problems in order to solve them.

Before I entered the Army, I never could understand why or how anyone could think other than the way I did. I knew nothing of broken homes, crime, etc. I had never known poverty or suffered child abuse from my parents. I hadn't lived in a cocoon, but I had grown up in a relatively safe environment. At the same time, I wasn't handed things arbitrarily—I had to work for them. At the time, I often thought that my parents were too strict because they made me do chores at home and they made me study in school. They also made me take music lessons and forced me to think on my own.

Before I entered the Service, I had only been out of the United States once in my life. I had taken a trip to the Bahamas. That little vacation didn't exactly prepare me for what I would see in Mexico, Japan, and Korea. After visiting some of these places during my time in the Army I came to realize how blessed I am to be an American. We have the best of everything available to us in this country. This is truly the land of opportunity. We have our problems too. We still struggle with race relations, poverty, crime, drugs, terrorists, undocumented aliens, and a whole slew of things that don't have simple solutions. But all in all, it's not too bad living in this country. Yes, we have high gasoline prices, high taxes, political corruption, and unemployment. Our education system is substandard and it leaves kids behind. The banking and insurance industries are out of control with no solution in sight.

We as Americans are overweight and are up to our ears in credit card debt. We have people living on welfare from generation to generation. We have elected officials who hide the truth and constantly barrage us with their individual agendas. We have lawyers who advertise on TV how to declare bankruptcy and get out of debt the easy way. We have doctors who spend more time worrying about getting sued for mistakes than they do curing people of their health problems. We have crooked cops and clergymen who take advantage of little kids. We have pornography all over the place. Divorces and suicides in this country are probably at an all-time high.

At the same time, we also have wonderful hospitals, clinics, grocery stores, and pharmacies on every corner, beautiful new schools, interstate highways, 24-hour banking, ATM's, cell phones, digital TV's, air-conditioning, clean water, sewage treatment plants, heat in the winter,

SUV's, boats, snow mobiles, mountain bikes, and motor homes. We go freely and without fear to wherever we want to go. We have beautiful national parks, water parks, amusement parks, and wonderful venues for watching professional sports. We have security, we have police and fire departments to protect us from the bad guys, we have paramedics to save our lives, and we have civil defense programs that warn us in advance of natural disasters. We live in a country that is blessed with almost endless resources. We all live, for the most part, in safe housing. We consume government-inspected food and approved drugs for our health needs. Things could be a lot worse. Most of the other countries around the world do not share in our prosperity.

Before entering the Army, I never really gave all of this too much thought. I just assumed and took for granted that all of these wonderful things were a normal part of life. I had no idea that other places around the world did not have this available for their people. Yes, I had studied these other countries in school, but until you visit these places you don't realize how much better off we are in this country compared to the way people live elsewhere. Culture shock is a mild understatement!

Americans get to vote for the people running our government. If we become dissatisfied with our leaders we can vote them out in the next election. The President can't just raise the taxes we pay every year on his own. Congress has to approve his budget proposal. It's not a perfect system by any stretch of the imagination, but at least we have some say in what goes on in our lives. The President can't just do whatever he or she feels like with our rights of privacy. The judicial system we have in place protects our rights that are spelled out in our nation's Constitution. We are free to pursue life, liberty, and happiness in just about any way we choose to do it. We can freely think what we want and speak out publicly to whoever will listen to us. We can even protest in an orderly and peaceful fashion about things we disagree with that our government gets involved in around the world.

We had a lot of this kind of activity going on back in the '70s. Protests against our involvement in Vietnam were quite prevalent back in those days. We are witnessing this again today as we continue to find our Service men and women in all parts of the world attempting to keep the peace. Our system of government allows for protest and disagreement if we so choose. They only require that we do it in a peaceful manner and that we don't infringe on others' rights to think as they might choose.

In my inadequate knowledge of the past and present history of the world, there are very few countries that allow totally free-thinking and public speaking about the issues at hand. In some countries where military dictators or religious leaders rule the masses, people can be put in prison, tortured, or even shot for thinking on their own or disagreeing with what their government is doing. In most of these cases, the people in these countries don't even have a say in who is running their government in the first place. They are forced to go along with whatever the government wants to do, like it or not.

There are many countries in the world today that are in such an economic and cultural mess that ethnic genocide and killing of innocent men, women, and children happens daily. There are many places in this world where even going to the market is dangerous. Religious and political fanatics throughout the world continue to blow up buildings and people without remorse simply to press forward their agendas and cause anarchy. These people don't want peace and stability in their countries. If that occurs no one will listen to them or read their propaganda.

Many countries around the world have long histories of existence for hundreds and in some cases, thousands of years. Their cultures are rich with tradition, and their religious beliefs go back to the beginnings of civilization. The United States of America has been around for a mere 240 years or so. This is a very short time in the annals of world history. Yes, we are probably the most advanced country the world has ever seen. But so were the Egyptians, the Greeks, and the Romans during their days of glory. And what about the Aztecs and the Mayans? What about the history of the Chinese and the Japanese cultures? These civilizations and their histories make our short existence seem like it is still in its infancy.

Is democracy the right way to go? Is belief in God as Christianity professes it correct? Are we Americans the "chosen people" to lead the rest of the world? Should we Americans involve ourselves with other people's problems? Is it up to America to straighten out everything in the world? Do we indeed have the right to do these things through our belief in Manifest Destiny? These are all good questions. None have easy answers. Only time will tell. All I know is that I, as one individual among millions, believe that I am living in the best place that I have ever seen or been to in my time on earth. Our country isn't perfect, but it's not too bad!

On September 11, 2001, the United States, as strong and powerful as it is, found out that it is vulnerable to attack from those who disagree with our point of view. We found out that there are people in this world who do not like our way of life and do not believe in our government. They continually threaten our security and our freedom. In their minds they would like to see the United States fall on its face in their efforts to keep the world at peace. Imagine that! How could anyone not see how prosperous we are as a people? Why can't they understand how well Democracy can work? Don't these people want to have the best things that life has to offer? These are all good questions, but once again they all have complex answers.

My wife and I visited Hawaii a couple of years ago. One of the highlights of our trip was our visit to Pearl Harbor. It was one of the most sobering and somber experiences of my life. As a veteran of the Army, it was one of my lifetime goals to visit this historic place. I would also like to someday visit the cemeteries in Europe and the Vietnam War memorial in Washington D.C. As an American citizen, I feel honor-bound to pay homage and salute to all of those servicemen and women who have died for this country. Without their ultimate sacrifice we would not be enjoying this wonderful country with all of its freedoms and liberties. I in no way pretend to think that my limited time in the Service even compares to what they did. I simply did my duty as a citizen, and when I was called upon to serve my country I did. I wasn't a hero or anything like that. I simply did my job to the best of my abilities. I am proud of what I accomplished while I was in the Army, and I am a proud and patriotic veteran. I believe that our country needs to maintain a strong military, and we must do what we can to keep our freedoms and liberties.

We live in a very unstable and dynamic time in our history. I am also certain that in the future, we as Americans will have more and more challenges to face. I can only hope that our children and future generations can keep our way of life intact as well as our forefathers have done in the past. I think every citizen in this country should make a trip to Mount Rushmore and gaze upon the sculptures of George Washington, Thomas

Jefferson, Teddy Roosevelt, and Abraham Lincoln. These visionary people began something that we must all protect and continue for posterity.

Wearing "That Shade of Green" for a short time during my life has definitely affected me in many ways. I still wear my hair short. I still make sure that the seams on my shirts are in line with the seams of my pants. I still make sure my shoes are shined. I shave almost every day. I even have a fondness for green-colored and khaki-colored clothing. I still get up early every morning. I still occasionally mix a Korean word or two into my vocabulary.

Thirty-nine years later, I still have two dress uniform jackets in my closet and my windbreaker from the Battery golf team. They don't fit me anymore, but I still have them. I still have my tankard from the "Last Rites Ceremony." Somewhere in my archives, I also have copies of the numerous articles that I wrote for *The Gauntlet* and the *Pacific Stars and Stripes* newspapers. I have a few slides and pictures of my escapades with my friend Thumper. But I mostly have memories. It was a time in my life that I will never forget, and I would gladly do it again if the opportunity presented itself.

I can't remember all of their names or where they were all from, and I'm not even sure today how many of them are even alive. This is one of my regrets in life that I didn't stay in touch with more of the guys that I met during this time. This is probably one of the driving forces behind my writing this story. Even though I can't remember all of their names, I can certainly say that the 19 months or so that I spent in the Army brought with it many memories of the guys who shared this experience with me. It is my hope that if any of them remember me, that they will get some enjoyment out of my view of the U.S. Army and the people that were a part of this organization in the early 1970s.

I would like to dedicate this book to my three children, who have encouraged me for years to finish it. I would also like to dedicate this book to the many thousands of servicemen and women who have died serving this country, as well as the thousands of Armed Service personnel presently serving around the world on our behalf. May God protect them and return them to their loved ones. I want them to come home just like I got to come home.

www.ingramcontent.com/pod-product-compliance
Lightning Source LLC
Chambersburg PA
CBHW031838090426
42741CB00005B/280